WHEN A Mom
Inspires HER
Daughter

CINDI McMENAMIN

HARVEST HOUSE PUBLISHERS
EUGENE, OREGON

Cover by Franke Design and Illustration, Excelsior, Minnesota

Cover photo © sarahwolfephotography / Flickr / Getty Images

WHEN A MOM INSPIRES HER DAUGHTER
Copyright © 2013 by Cindi McMenamin
Published by Harvest House Publishers
Eugene, Oregon 97402
www.harvesthousepublishers.com

Library of Congress Cataloging-in-Publication Data
McMenamin, Cindi, 1965-
When a mom inspires her daughter / Cindi McMenamin.
  pages cm
Includes bibliographical references.
ISBN 978-0-7369-5453-2 (pbk.)
ISBN 978-0-7369-5454-9 (eBook)
1. Mothers and daughters—Religious aspects—Christianity. 2. Daughters—Religious life. 3. Teenage girls—Religious life. 4. Christian teenagers—Religious life. I. Title.
BV4529.18.M38 2013
248.8'431—dc23
                                                                            2013002889

Printed in the United States of America

13 14 15 16 17 18 19 20 21 / BP-JH / 10 9 8 7 6 5 4 3 2 1

When a Mom Inspires Her Daughter

Not only is Cindi McMenamin a spiritual and practical encourager of women around the globe, but she is a friend. I am especially thrilled by this latest book aimed at the hearts of moms. Nothing is more important for a mom with girls than teaching them God's standards and modeling how to follow them…and never has the challenge been so critical. This book is timely and an answer to every mother's prayers for help with preparing her daughter for life.

—Elizabeth George
Author of *A Woman After God's Own Heart*

"Drawing on her own considerable experience as a mother and mentor, as well as conducting extensive interviews with women who both mentor and have been mom-mentored, Cindi McMenamin has put together a practical, readable, hands-on manual on relating to your daughter or daughter-in-law. A great gift for a new mommy or longtime mother, this book will also be particularly useful to mothers and daughters whose relationship is thorny or broken."

—Rebekah Binkley Montgomery
Author of *Faithprints: Touching Your World for Jesus*

"Too many mothers back away right when their daughters need—and crave—their involvement and guidance. In *When a Mom Inspires Her Daughter*, Cindi offers practical encouragement for being intentional in living out our irreplaceable roles as mature mentors to our daughters. And she challenges us to recognize that because our girls are most influenced by who we are (and not merely by what we say or by who we wish we were), living in Christ's love is our most important—and inspiring—priority."

—Cheri Gregory
Mother of an adult daughter, 20+ year veteran
of junior high and high school teaching, and coauthor of
The Good Girls' Guide to Breaking Bad Rules

"In your hands is a *treasure trove* of reflective wisdom, a keepsake journal to capture your heart's cry and delight, and a compilation of insight for seeking answers as a mother of a daughter. Regardless of how you feel about the woman who raised you or your feelings about how you did, are doing, or will do raising your daughter; she reminds us we were "chosen over every other woman in this world to be our daughter's mom." Sobering, yes, but a gift for certain!"

—Barbara Willett
Board member, Network of Evangelical
Women in Ministry, Redondo Beach, CA

For my mom, Joyce:
As I've focused on how to be an inspirational mother to my daughter,
I was continually reminded —and thankful—of the many ways
you were absolutely remarkable as a mom. Thank you for encour-
aging me, inspiring me, and doing all you could to see me develop
wings and fly.

For my stepmom, Sharon:
You have loved me as your own. And for that I will always be grate-
ful. Thank you for your extremely generous heart in so many ways.

And for my daughter, Dana:
I can't imagine how different—and uneventful—life would be if
you weren't living it alongside me. It has been a joy to watch you
grow and develop into a godly, courageous young woman who is
not afraid to follow her dreams. My prayer is that you will continue
to soar and that I will always be someone you look to as your
closest friend.

Acknowledgments

My heartfelt thanks to:

- The many moms who shared their wisdom, as well as what they wish they'd done better so other moms could learn from their mistakes.
- The many daughters who shared their insights and, in some cases, heartaches, so moms can learn from what you have to say.
- My sister, Kristi Foss, for her timely words at a crucial time when I was raising my daughter.
- My husband, Hugh, for his unconditional love and patience during long hours as I wrote another book.
- My daughter, Dana, for being the inspiration behind this book.
- My editor, Steve Miller, and the publishing committee at Harvest House Publishers for supporting me in another book to encourage women.

And above all, I'm grateful to my Lord and Savior Jesus Christ, who modeled sacrificial love to me so that I could, by His grace and strength, model it to my daughter.

Contents

The Beauty—and Burden— of Raising a Daughter

Oh, to be able to hear your daughter one day say, "My mom is everything I want to be in a woman."

Sure, you might get that in a Mother's Day or birthday card now and then. But in your heart of hearts you are asking the same soul-searching questions that so many other mothers ask, including me: *Am I influencing her in the best possible way I can? Am I really doing all I can to be there for her? Is she adopting the insecurities and weaknesses I have? Am I showing her a proper picture of God's love in the way I relate to her on a daily basis?*

A woman in my church has a preschool daughter and has asked those questions. A close friend of mine has a 16-year-old daughter and, when the relationship gets volatile, she asks those questions as well. My daughter has entered her twenties and I still ask myself if I'm living out my faith in a way that is real and influential. And there are women I speak to around the country who have daughters in their thirties and forties whom they still very much want to influence positively and, in some cases, draw back to God's heart.

If you're like these mothers, there is so much you want to instill in your daughter's life, and yet there are so many things you feel you *should* be doing, but aren't. In a world of dismal statistics on divorce; growing cases of depression among women;[1] an alarming increase in eating disorders;[2] and the increasing need for therapists, medication, and counseling for any number of syndromes; our concern for our daughters—and their daughters—is understandable. And yet you have been put in a position to make a difference in her life that no one else can.

When you first held your daughter in your hands, you were aware, I'm sure, of the tremendous blessing that she was. You were probably amazed at how instantly she wrapped herself around your heart. And your heart has not been the same since. And yet, as you hold this book in your hands right now, you may well understand the *burden* of raising her that comes with that blessing. It's a responsibility you don't want to take lightly. It's a weight that never leaves your shoulders. It's a privilege, yet a downright scary one at times. And you have probably experienced days—and maybe you still do—during which you weren't sure if you were up to the task at all.

But, my friend, there is a beauty in that burden of raising a young woman who is so much like and yet so different from you. There is an incredible privilege in being the one person in the world with the ability (whether you've recognized it or not) to connect with her heart at levels you still might not understand.

That daughter of yours, whether born from your body or attained through the grace of God, is a gift on loan from God, who appointed you, over any other individual on this earth, to be her mother. And with that great privilege of mothering your daughter comes great responsibility.

I realize that you might, at this point, be wondering if you have much influence left. Maybe your little girl is grown up, set in her ways, and determined to live the way she wants. Or maybe the influence you once had as a mom seems to be dwindling now that your daughter is getting older and wanting her independence. You may even feel that, at times, she wants nothing to do with you. But, it's never too late to relight that match of inspiration in your daughter's heart and be the kind of mom she's always needed.

Let me assure you, first of all, by saying this: You are not where you are by chance. You're the mom of a daughter (and maybe God has even blessed you with more than one!). And don't think for a moment that took

God by surprise. During the course of your mothering, God at no point regretted making you her mom. Psalm 18:30 says God's ways are perfect and therefore, He makes no mistakes.

In Scripture, we find these wonderful words written by the psalmist, who describes our significance and our destiny in the hands of an all-knowing, all-seeing God:

> My frame was not hidden from you when I was made in the secret place, when I was woven together in the depths of the earth. Your eyes saw my unformed body; all the days ordained for me were written in your book before one of them came to be (Psalm 139:15-16).

That verse tells me that just as your daughter's body was woven intricately in her mother's womb (and in your heart) and her life was planned out in detail by God, *you,* being her mother, were woven intricately by God in *your* mother's womb as well. And the fact that you would be that little girl's (or young woman's) mother was also planned out by God before you were ever born.

Nothing has given me more confidence than to know that my daughter was not an accident. Nor was the fact that I was chosen to be her mom. And the same goes for you. That's right—*you* were *chosen*, over every other woman in this world, to be your daughter's mom.

What If I've Done a Lousy Job?

I realize you might be feeling, at this point, that so far you're doing a lousy job. There might be friction between you and your daughter, or you might be carrying feelings of guilt over not being there for her as much as you'd like. Or maybe you've done all you can, but your daughter's heart seems to be hardening against you. Believe me, every mother in the world feels, at times, that she has done a lousy job. And nearly every mother I surveyed for this book has, at one time or another, believed her daughter wanted nothing to do with her. But, likewise, we all believe there is still a lot we have to learn. And there is hope in the fact that you desire to inspire her to live a life of purpose and passion; to affirm her identity and her dreams; to be her encouragement, support, and mentor. And you *will* be (if you're not already). I'm certain of it.

My Own Hesitancy

I'll be the first to admit I never pictured myself as a mom. And I certainly didn't ever believe I'd be a good one. I wasn't the babysitting, baby-crooning, bootie-crocheting type of woman at all. I had wanted to push an agenda, not a stroller. I wanted a career, not a child.

But the day came when my maternal instincts took over and I wanted a daughter to hold, love, and raise. That's right—my first thought, when I considered having a child, was that I wanted a baby *girl.*

But, after nine long months of all-day sickness (do some women experience only *morning* sickness?), fourteen hours of labor, three hours of pushing, and finally an emergency C-section, there weren't many happy moments associated with the pregnancy and delivery of my first child... until I heard the elating announcement, "It's a girl!"

Throughout my pregnancy, my husband, Hugh, had insisted that we not find out the gender of our first child so it would be a surprise. ("To find out ahead of time would be like opening our presents *before* Christmas," Hugh kept saying.) I went along with his suggestion halfheartedly, yet there were many times I wished I could find out our child's gender for the sake of decorating her room, buying baby clothes, and so on. But I'm so grateful now for Hugh's decision for us to wait. That announcement, that I finally had my much-wanted baby *girl,* was the redeeming moment of my whole experience of carrying and birthing a child.

When I arrived home from the hospital with baby Dana, there were pink curly ribbons on our front door and all over the inside of our house, thanks to my former college roommate and neighbor, Christi, who pretty much walked me through my pregnancy, delivery, and those first few years.

Christi, too, had hoped for a little girl for me. I never had a younger sister. My older sister had two sons. My parents didn't yet have a grand-daughter, and there was a shortage of little girls on my husband's side of the family as well. It was high time for a little girl in the family. And my husband and I got her: Dana Katherine McMenamin. What a blessing!

I didn't know then that she would be the only child I would be able to have. That she would be such a central figure in our home, our marriage, my spiritual growth, and the development of my character. That she would present her share of challenges yet bring to us unspeakable joy. But I can honestly say that through the ups and downs—from days when I know that she didn't like me very much and I loathed her attitude to days I believed I was the worst parent ever, especially to a girl—she and I, today, are the best of friends. The ins and outs of parenting a daughter was worth it all. The tears I shed when I asked God for wisdom in raising her were not wasted. God is faithful. And I can think of no greater blessing today than to be the mom of a daughter.

When the Task Looks Daunting

Maybe that's not exactly how you feel right now. If so, I understand that. A mother-daughter relationship can be challenging, especially during her teenage and early adult years. If she's just like you, the two of you will clash at times. If she's unlike you, you'll misunderstand each other. But when you understand that the clashes and chaos, the drama and disappointments can work to bring you and your daughter into a closer relationship with God and with each other, that can make all the difficulties more bearable.

Your daughter is not a clone of you. She is her own person. She is created uniquely in the image of God. She has some strengths like you. She bears some weaknesses like you. She has some annoying traits that are unlike you, and some that resemble you to a T. In no other situation in life are we as mothers called to love, serve, train, shape, discipline, and develop another woman who is so much like us yet so different from us. The task is daunting and, at times, scary. But it can also be tremendously rewarding.

I would like to give you hope and inspiration through some tools in this book that, prayerfully, will begin drawing your daughter's heart closer to yours. As you begin to see her as God's unique creation and your friend and sister in Christ, the doorway will open wider to delighting in her and becoming a blessing in her life.

What's in Store?

Throughout this book we will look at ways in which we've been shaped as mothers and ways we can help shape our daughters to become the best women, wives, and mothers they can be. We will look at some of the challenging aspects of mothering a daughter, and the areas in which your daughter needs you to provide encouragement, support, inspiration, and gentle guidance. Along the way, you will read thoughts from my daughter, Dana, and hear from other mothers and daughters who share their wisdom and insights about what has drawn them to each other's hearts. Each chapter will conclude with some thought questions for you to reflect on and some practical exercises so you can apply the principles discussed. Each chapter also ends with a prayer to strengthen your mother-daughter relationship.

So, yes, this book is for you...

- whether your daughter is in elementary school or has elementary school children of her own
- whether she lives with you or is half the country—or half the world—away
- whether the two of you talk every day or haven't talked in a while
- whether you feel you've done a great job with her or feel you've completely blown it

Just the fact that you've picked up this book and started reading it tells me your heart's desire is to draw her closer to you. And I applaud your desire. So let me encourage you as you embark on this journey.

First Corinthians 13:7-8 tells us that love "bears all things, believes all things, hopes all things, and endures all things. Love never fails."[3]

As long as you have a heart to love, encourage, and affirm your daughter, no matter what her age, you will not fail. Because no matter how young or old your daughter is, no matter how many of them you have, no matter how good or bad the status of your relationship, it's never too early—or too late—to start affirming her identity and her dreams.

A Prayer for the Journey Ahead

God, grant me the wisdom and desire, from this point forward, to be the best mother I can be for the young woman—or women—You have put in my life. No matter what has happened, or what will happen, may I always see my daughter as a blessing from Your hand, a heart on loan, a gift from Your heart to mine. Bless her life at this moment, Lord, and may she know with all her being that she is precious to me. Begin a work in her heart right now as you begin a work in mine. And may You draw our hearts closer toward one another and closer toward You.

Chapter 1

Your Amazing Ability to Influence

Let love and faithfulness never leave you;
bind them around your neck,
write them on the tablet of your heart.

PROVERBS 3:3

I will study your teachings and follow your footsteps.

PSALM 119:15 CEV

As you hold this book in your hands, you may be thinking it's all about your daughter. But really, this book is all about *you*. It's about the responsibility *you've* been given—recently or years ago—to raise a woman who loves God and others. It's about the opportunity *you* have to influence her in ways that no one else can. And it's about the amazing ability within *you* to be the most powerful human force and inspiration in her life.

We are all influenced by *someone*. Friends, teachers, leaders, television celebrities, and musicians all compete for the strongest influence in your daughter's life. Yet from the time she was born (or from the day she was put into your care), you were planted in that role of being her primary influencer. You, her mom, start out as the single most influential person in her life...until the day she might decide to look elsewhere for a role model.

No matter how young or old your daughter is, realize that it's never too early or too late to start inspiring her. *You* can be the one person she looks to, over anyone else, for advice, approval, encouragement, and inspiration—even during her teen years. Even during her adult years.

We are often the first person our daughters strive to imitate as they are growing up and learning about the world. If you have a preschooler or elementary school-aged daughter, you know what I mean. She hangs on to your every word, and perhaps onto your legs too! She wants to be with you and like you. She thrills your heart as she, in some ways, is your mini-me. But if you have a teenager you might be thinking, *What? She doesn't even want me around!*

Your role as influencer, role model, and mentor in her life is still there, however, whether she acts like she appreciates it or not. And if you feel by now that you have lost that influence and potential to be her inspiration, I want to help you, through the rest of this book, to get that back.

Our Silent Example

A very humbling aspect of motherhood is the realization that our daughters are watching and imitating a lot of what we do, whether we want them to or not. Our girls pick up not just our loving, positive, and productive behaviors, but our mistakes, dysfunctions, and insecurities as well.

Annemarie, a 21-year-old college student who sings her mother's praises, admitted that she had become a perfectionist and one who is very hard on herself—not because her mom was hard on her, but because of traits she saw in her mom and what she assumed her mom was thinking about her.

"My mom was always a hard worker, and she set such high expectations for herself and was constantly trying so hard that I thought she must want me to be the exact same way," Annemarie said. "However, I wasn't the same person she was. I didn't feel comfortable there. If she expected perfect, I was sure to be a consistent disappointment. I never said so, but I did not desire to be perfect. I liked imperfections—I liked the flaws I found in things. I thought they made them so much more interesting. It meant possibility, potential. So I was set up (I'm sure I set myself up more than she did) to fail even before I had gotten started. I had no interest in being perfect, but if Mom cared about it, surely I should. So when I didn't have a 4.0 GPA, or a cute boyfriend, or better eating habits, or a perfect understanding of precalculus, I would automatically feel guilty, ashamed, and defensive. Because my mom placed so much importance on being perfect, I felt like a failure as a daughter time after time after time.

"Although this was something I was aware of when I was younger, it didn't start to seriously affect my relationship with my mom until I reached high school. I am now in my second-to-last year of college, and I'm finally beginning to understand that my mother does not want or expect me to be her."

Annemarie's mom, Cheri, doesn't remember receiving any praise, acceptance, or affection from her own mother. Therefore, she naturally became an overachiever, trying hard to get her mother's approval and affection. And *because* Cheri never received encouragement or praise or acceptance from her mother, she poured these things out on her daughter, never realizing or imagining that her daughter would see it as pressure to perform.

"My mother was always at her wit's end with my messy room and crazy ideas (like wanting to take horseback riding lessons rather than practice piano)," Cheri said. "She couldn't understand why I would want to get on stage for drama. So although I got attention, it was mostly negative— I was told of all the things I wasn't doing that she thought I should. I received little approval and no affection that I can remember."

But since Cheri had a mom who wasn't intimately involved in her life, she strove to provide that aspect of mothering for Annemarie. In hindsight, she now wishes she had dealt with some of those childhood issues so she hadn't affected her daughter's life the way she did.

"I've recently become aware that I've meddled in my daughter's life too much, doing too much for her and making life too easy for her. So I've been trying to back away and detach without abandoning her. It's hard. I'm not as affectionate and touchy as she'd like me to be, but I lack good role-modeling in that area.

"I've also become aware, very recently, that I've sacrificed a lot in my life so that she can do whatever she wants and be happy...which is, of course, what I wish my mother had done with me. So when Annemarie went through severe anxiety and depression her freshman year of college, I was totally unprepared. After all I'd done for her, how could she *not* be happy? That was *all* I ever wanted for her. I didn't see how codependent I was being."

Our daughters are watching us, learning from us, imitating us in ways we might not even realize. That's why it's so important that we know who we are and who we want to be when it comes to influencing our daughters.

Who Are You, Really?

Whether your daughter is the light of your life right now or a daily challenge who is keeping you on your knees in prayer, understanding who she is and what makes her tick is essential to drawing her heart closer to yours and having a greater impact on her life.

But before you can understand who your daughter is and positively influence her, you must first know who *you* are. I'll say that again: You need to know who *you* are so you can help your daughter to know who *she* is. Here's why: Our daughters model our behavior in so many ways. They end up imitating both the positive and the negative in us. So, if you are constantly searching for your own identity, struggling for a sense of purpose or dealing with insecurities, chances are your daughter will too. We have to realize that when our daughters are young we are the primary *shapers* of their lives, and when they are older, we can serve as the primary *encouragers* in their lives.

Also, who you are today, as a mother, is in many ways shaped by who your own mother is—or was.

If that thought makes you smile, it's probably because you had a jewel of a mom who gave of herself sacrificially for you and you can only sing her praises. If that's the case, there are so many characteristics in her that you already want to imitate. And you are reading this book to find out even more ways you can be the kind of mom to your daughter that your mother was to you.

But if that thought doesn't make you smile, it's probably because recognizing the fact you are shaped or influenced by your own mother is somewhat of a painful matter for you. But please stick with me. My hope is this chapter will have a healing effect on you such that you let go of some of that hurt and embrace the positive qualities your mom had that you might not have recognized before.

As I surveyed moms and daughters for this book, I found it interesting that those who spoke most favorably about their moms were speaking in hindsight. Their mothers had passed away, and they were no longer able to enjoy a relationship with them. Is it because, after our mothers are gone, we are more able to appreciate their positive character traits? Is it because when we miss our moms we more readily remember the good things about them? If that's the case, and your mom is still alive, you can do your heart good by finding the positive aspects of her mothering *now* while she is still alive, so you don't have the heartache later of having never expressed to her your appreciation for what she instilled into you. I *know* you want your daughter to think only lovely thoughts about you, both now and when you've passed on. So bear with me, my friend, while we pull back the layers of our hearts to look at some of the ways we were positively impacted by our mothers. Trust me—just by going here with me, you may find healing for your heart, and possibly your daughter's too.

Finding the Positive

My mom was extremely creative. My brothers and sister and I always had the most original costumes for the town's annual holiday parades, the school plays, and friends' costume parties. Mom wrote and directed theatrical productions in town (and let us perform in them, alongside the adults, giving us valuable onstage experience that every one of us uses today in some aspect or another). She transformed our large backyard of dirt, grass, and a few fruit trees into a child's wonderland with a wading pond, a duck pond, a creek and bridge, a couple of decks, a tree house, greenhouse, bird aviaries, and even a nicely landscaped above-ground pool. Because I wanted to be a librarian someday, she built me a free-standing, wood-paneled, carpeted "library," complete with high ceilings and electricity, so I had a place to house all my books that I would loan out to my neighbors and friends as I played librarian. It was incredible what my mother could build, create, and accomplish. And she did all of that for her children. Looking back now, I realize that was pretty special. In fact, it was extraordinary.

I asked my sister, Kristi, to tell me what she remembers about Mom (to make sure I wasn't embellishing!) and this is what she said about how Mom influenced her:

"Mom modeled that a confident, strong woman could accomplish anything a man can. She was fearless when it came to tackling jobs outside her areas of expertise. If she set her mind to something she worked diligently until it was finished, and the results were always incredible. I watched her build a bird aviary, pour concrete to make a duck pond and waterfall, and build a deck and create a beautiful backyard for us kids to play in. If she didn't know how to do something, she would check out a book at the library (this was before the Internet, of course!), seek a professional and ask questions, or figure it out on her own. I was always amazed that she never considered a job too hard, too complicated, or out of her reach. She taught me to work hard, and if you could dream it, you could do it with hard work, and lots of sore muscles and iced tea."

I suppose it isn't any wonder that our mom raised four children who pursued their dreams: Kristi is a professional musician, voice teacher, and worship leader. I am an author and speaker. My brother, Dan, is a code breaker for the FBI; and my youngest brother, Steve, is a professional television animator/director.

A Perspective Change

With all that in mind, I'm saddened now to admit that for most of my early adult years, I focused more on what I perceived as my mother's faults than her strengths. Yet after my daughter became a teenager and started expressing a critical spirit toward me (interestingly, that was the same age at which I became critical toward my own mom), I realized just how hurtful that must have been to my mom and how very much I wanted my own daughter to overlook my weaknesses and focus on my strengths. This is when I realized that if I wanted to encourage Dana to see me in a positive light, I had to be a woman who, by example, saw her mother in a positive light as well. I needed to be a woman who praised, loved, and appreciated her mom in the same way I wanted to be praised, loved, and appreciated by my daughter. Now that I'm older and a mother myself, I am able to see my mom through different lenses, through more gracious lenses, through the lenses of a mother.

As I've aged (and especially now that I have a grown daughter of my own), I have extended more grace to my mom in those areas I felt she didn't do so well because I realize I am so capable of doing or not doing the very same things with my own daughter. I have also focused on the good things I've acquired from my mother and ways that I am happy to be like her because not only am I grateful to her for how she invested in my life, but also I want Dana to show grace to me someday. I want my daughter to see the good things I did, imitate what she liked in me, and remember where those positive traits came from. Most of all, I want her to cherish thoughts of her mother's love, inspiration, and support.

It's true we can make our mothers the brunt of endless jokes and cringe at the thought of becoming like them. But in reality, our mothers have shaped us far more than we will ever realize. And, like it or not, we, too, will shape what kind of women or mothers our daughters will become. Will our daughters laugh at our idiosyncrasies? Probably. But will they see all that we did was out of love and support for them too? Prayerfully.

While this book will focus primarily on your relationship with your daughter, one of the ways to begin having a healthy relationship with her is to release any resentment or bitterness you might have toward your mother.

Making Peace with Mom

We tend to believe we are either "just like my mom" or "nothing like my mom," but the truth is, we are all made up of *something* of our mothers. It's inevitable. Likewise, our daughters will, in many ways, be the product of us.

Take a moment right now to think about who you are as a woman and as a mother, and how you have been positively influenced by your mom. Are you compassionate because of how you saw her treat others? Are you ambitious because of what you've seen her accomplish? Are you creative or detail oriented because she was or wasn't? Do you love to cook because of what she taught you in the kitchen? Dig deep if you have to. Just as you would like your daughter to remember some positive things about you, what can you remember that is positive about your mother?

Quiet your heart right now. Ask God to give you a clear mind and open heart as you ponder the following statements. And please feel free to write out your answers in the space below if you are reading this in a print book. I believe you'll find it helpful to place your thoughts on paper.

My mother was good at:

My mother taught me to:

I am most like my mother in the following ways:

A Look at Your Legacy in the Making

Now try to answer the following questions from your daughter's perspective. (I will give you an opportunity to get her actual answers later; for now, write what you think and hope she would say.)

What would my daughter say that I excel at?

What would she say I have *taught* her to do?

In what ways would I like my daughter to say she is a lot like me?

What do I hope my daughter will remember most about me after I die?

If you're like me, when you answered the questions about your mom, doing so may have opened your eyes to the power of her influence over you, possibly without you even realizing it. And when you answered the questions about your daughter, doing so may have made you think about your priorities in life and what she is seeing *right now*. While you may not want to think about your daughter coping with losing you one day, how she will remember you is something to keep in mind while you can still impact her answers. She is watching the way you are living now. And she is being impacted by the ways you respond—or don't respond—to her.

In the interviews I conducted before writing this book, many women said something to the effect of "My mom changed a lot during my adult years, and we are the best of friends today." That can still happen with you and your daughter just in case you're thinking it might be too late to influence what she says or remembers about you. And the fact that you are taking the time to read this book now convinces me that you are willing to do what you can to make your relationship a positive one that gives her good memories of your influence.

As you gain peace in your heart about your mother, you can better become the kind of mom your daughter needs. She needs you whole and at peace so that she can be too. When you are struggling to forgive your mom, or harboring resentment in your heart at how you were raised, that bitterness will show up in ways you may not realize or expect. That, in turn, could impact your daughter.

I also know many daughters who absolutely adore their maternal grandmother yet find it difficult to express their feelings around their mother because of a past falling-out between Mom and Grandma. Don't make your daughter suffer through that. Don't force her to compartmentalize her heart. Let her know you love your mom (even if it's an "after she's gone, I've forgiven her" type of love), and your daughter will feel free to love her too.

Learning from Past Pain

Sadly, Tina, a 30-year-old mother of a 14-year-old daughter, still feels resentment toward her mother today. Having been physically and verbally abused by her alcoholic/addict mother, she says to this day her mother isn't able to forget about herself and encourage her daughter or granddaughter.

Being a single mom, perhaps Tina needed that love and encouragement from her own mother even more, but she didn't receive it. By contrast, she is determined to give her daughter, Marie, a different life than she herself had while growing up by focusing on communicating and showing affection toward her.

"I try hard to make sure she can talk to me about anything," Tina said. "I also communicate openly with her and answer her questions honestly. She receives love best with quality time, so I make sure we have regular mother-daughter time. She knows I'll always be there for her."

If you are a woman with hurtful memories about your mother, pray that God will release from you any bitterness that has taken hold in your heart. And ask God to show you, through past hurts, how to be for your daughter what you always wanted in a mother—how to give in areas in which you were not given to, how to love in ways you were not loved, and how to offer to your daughter something different and far better than you experienced. God has an amazing ability to redeem the hurtful things you've experienced and work them for good in your life and in the lives of others.[4]

Do you see your daughter relating to you in a similar way that you related to your own mom? If so, that can give you insight into her heart. For instance, when Dana was a preteen and young teenager we clashed in the ways we responded to each other. When I sensed a frustration in her voice as she tried to talk with me, it reminded me of the frustration I experienced when I tried to talk to my mom about situations we saw differently. I remember thinking I was so right, so misunderstood, so unfairly treated in certain moments when I was a teenager. Could Dana have been feeling the same toward me?

Upon recognizing (and relating to) Dana's frustration, I took the opportunity, immediately, to say, "Dana, I know you feel frustrated right now. I remember feeling this way with my own mom. There are some things you will probably not understand until you are my age and you have a daughter yourself. But until then, please trust me that I love you and want what's best for you." And then I remembered—it was words similar to those, spoken by my own mom, that calmed my heart during similarly tense moments when I was growing up.

As a mom, you need to remember how you related to your own mother, what frustrated you, what you wished she had done differently, and what spoke love to your heart. And use those memories to help you relate in a more loving way to your daughter.

Appreciating Her Uniqueness

Since I was so excited to have a little girl, in many ways I expected Dana to be just like me. And she seemed to start out that way. But as she grew, I saw her developing personality traits that were, well, more like those of her father. That was fine, but did she have to develop the specific traits that I had difficulty understanding and relating to? Yet as Dana has grown into a young woman, I have come to appreciate those traits more. Just as my closest girlfriends are in many ways different from me, Dana's differences balance me out. And I learn from her. In fact, in some ways, I strive to be more like her rather than the other way around.

I asked Dana to list the ways she is like me and the ways she is unlike me so I could get a better idea of how she sees the two of us in terms of our similarities and differences. It was fun to see her perspective on this and she brought out a couple of similarities and differences about us that I didn't realize existed. (She also opened my eyes to some of the ways I have influenced her without realizing it.) Here is what Dana came up with (and my responses in parentheses):

Ways I'm like my mom:	Ways I'm unlike my mom:
We both like to shop (and we both love a good bargain!).	I can only shop for an hour… she can shop for four!
We both like only ketchup and mayo on our burgers.	My dad and I love sushi…my mom freaks out at the sight of it.
We are both very over-dramatic (yes, those were Dana's words).	My mom loves pink…I hate pink.
We both love to dress with style.	I used to love leopard print… now my mom wears it! (Ok, not so much anymore.)
We are both well organized.	
We both don't cook…unless it's boxed macaroni. ("Oh dear," the mom says!)	I love the 1950s…my mom loves the 1980s.
We both love to decorate.	My dad and I love comedy shows, particularly *Saturday Night Live*…my mother doesn't understand it.
We both love to write (Mom has a BIG smile here!).	
We both take time to look good —with our hair, makeup, nails.	My dad and I love action/adventure movies…my mom likes romantic movies.
We both like to eat…a lot.	My dad and I like to sleep…my mom could stay up all night.
We both plan out our day/week on a sheet of paper.	My dad and I don't like parties… my mom loves parties.
	I am more daring than my mom. I'd do a back handspring without her knowing. (What???)
	My mom is high energy; I am more laid back.

In looking over Dana's lists, I see some likes that were probably ingrained in her (a love for writing?) and some that she probably learned by watching me (making to-do lists every day, I'm sure). I also see some traits that come from her father (that would be the introvert in her and her taste for sushi). But looking at the second list also makes me smile. I love the fact she isn't just like me. And her interests have stretched me and opened me up to new interests, experiences, and adventures. In fact, the clothes Dana picks out for me are not ones I would pick out for myself, but they often end up being my favorite—and the most practical pieces of clothing in my closet!

················· From Her Perspective ·················

"We Are More Alike than We'd Like to Admit"

Dana had some interesting thoughts about the similarities between moms and daughters in general:

"We daughters are a lot like our moms, no matter how hard we try to make it seem like we're not.

"One of the ways we are influenced by our moms—and therefore a lot like them—is in our motherly instincts. How our mothers respond and act toward us helps shape how we respond and act toward others. For example, the way that my mother cares for others has shown up in me as well. When I see a baby, I want to hold that baby and care for it. And the way my mother gives me advice has influenced the way I give advice to my friends and peers.

"Another way we can tend to be like our mothers is in the area of our emotions. Even though our personalities are different—my mother is an extrovert and I am an introvert—we still have the same emotions when it comes to certain issues; we just express them differently. When my mother is upset, she will let her feelings out and want to talk about it or cry. When I am upset, I don't talk to anyone and I very rarely cry. But I still feel the emotion as strongly as she does—I just react to it in a different way.

"I think one reason mothers and daughters have a difficult time dealing with certain issues is because one will want to talk about it and the other won't. When mothers and daughters are alike, they can tend to clash, especially if they are both strong-willed and independent, and each wants to get their message across first. Also, if they are both having their periods, then everything is magnified ten times over! Women are naturally emotional, so for two women to come together and work things out can get difficult sometimes. And between a mother and daughter it can get especially challenging!

"One particular challenge is that daughters can be different than their moms expect because of the way they are like their fathers. Mothers don't have genes and personality traits from their husbands, but their daughters do. So mothers will start to see traits of the father in their child. In my case, I have my dad's sense of humor and introverted personality. When I make a joke, sometimes my mother doesn't understand and gets offended, whereas my dad will laugh it off and joke along with me. Sometimes mothers don't understand why their daughters act so differently from them, but one reason is because the father helped make the child too. A child is going to have traits from *both* mom and dad, so she is going to be different...something the mother won't always understand because she doesn't possess those traits. The mom simply marries the man, but the child has his DNA!

"Bottom line is, no matter how hard we try to steer away from being just like our mothers, we are probably going to grow up very much like them, but with our own unique personality and character traits. When I was younger I would roll my eyes and scoff when someone told me I was like my mother. But today when someone tells me, 'You look just like your mother' or 'You and your mother act the same when it comes to this,' I now take that as a compliment."

When They Want to Be Like Us

Every little girl, at one time or another, dreams of growing up and being like her mom. I remember when Dana loved wearing matching dresses with me. (I have pictures of every time we did that!) Today, I would love it if she would still wear matching outfits with me. But now that she's an adult, that's not likely. In fact, she gets a look of horror on her face if she notices we are going out the door to church together wearing similar clothes or styles and she doesn't have time to change. ("Really, Mom? Do you have to dress just like me?") Just like any young woman, it's very important to my daughter that she look like herself, not a clone of her mother.

While it's flattering when our little girls want to become like us someday, it can backfire on us too. As it did in Janet Thompson's case.

Janet recommitted her life to the Lord in her forties, after 17 years of backsliding and influencing her daughter's priorities and behavior more than she expected. Because Janet made such a drastic turnaround in her life after receiving Christ as her personal Savior, she assumed her daughter would imitate her right living. Yet Janet was shocked one day when she heard her preteen daughter, Kim, describe her ideal plans for her life—plans that included most of her mother's mistakes prior to her salvation.

"I then realized my daughter had watched me and wanted to become like me. But she wanted to imitate the old me, not the new, regenerated me," Janet said. "It broke my heart that the woman she wanted to emulate was the one who had done all the damage." (More of this story—including how God worked in Kim's heart—is told in chapter 9.)

Today Janet, who is the author of *Woman to Woman Mentoring* as well as other books, including *Praying for Your Prodigal Daughter*, tells women to "*be* the woman you want your daughter to become."[5]

That's what this book is going to help you do. In the next chapter we'll look at how to identify what your daughter needs. Then throughout the rest of this book, we will look at how you can nurture her, give her the gift of your time, enter her world, encourage her dreams, and prepare her for life. We'll also look at how to choose your battles wisely so your relationship with her is not lived on a battlefield. And finally, we'll look at how you can guide her spiritually and earn her respect so you can be her best friend through her adult years. All the while, in learning these things, you will find yourself practicing godly womanhood. *You* will be developing into the woman you want *her* to be. So let's get started.

Getting God's Help

As we start our journey together, let's make sure we seek God's input along the way. When we ask God for the wisdom to become the kind of mom our daughters need, we want to make sure we do the following:

1. We Must Ask According to His Will

First John 5:14 says that to ask for something in Jesus' name (or to ask for something "according to his will") means to ask God the Father for something Jesus would ask for. Is your request for God's glory or for your own? Are you asking on behalf of Jesus, or for your own selfish gain?

When young Solomon was crowned king of Israel, God gave him an incredible offer: "Ask for whatever you want me to give you" (1 Kings 3:5). Wow! Can you imagine that? God giving you carte blanche? Solomon could have asked anything of God and received it. He could've asked for riches. He could've asked for fame. He could've asked for a life of pleasure and no pain. Yet he asked for something that pleased God's heart. He asked for wisdom to rule God's people the right way. He said, "More than anything, God, I need the ability to rule the people You have placed under my care. I want to do You right."

Solomon apparently felt the weight of responsibility on his shoulders. Not only was he the new king of Israel, but he was following in the footsteps of his father, David, a king who had been larger-than-life. David would forever be known as Israel's greatest, most beloved king. Solomon was attempting to fill the shoes of a legend. And he must have felt very inadequate, very ill-prepared, very humbled.

Do you ever feel like that? If you are raising a headstrong teenager, you might feel like that. If you've felt you are lacking the skills needed to be a mom or you've felt you didn't have a good role model when it came to mothering, you may feel like that.

Remarkably, Solomon's request for God to give him the wisdom he lacked was honored by God in ways Solomon hadn't dreamed. God not only gave young Solomon the wisdom he needed to rule His people (and a legacy of being the wisest man who ever lived), He also gave Solomon fame and riches that he *didn't* ask for.[6]

When you desire to raise your daughter in a positive way that honors God, you are asking for something that God would want you to ask for. That is a desire that pleases God's heart.

2. We Must Ask in Faith

In James 1:6-7 we are told that when we ask for wisdom we "must believe and not doubt, because the one who doubts is like a wave of the sea, blown and tossed by the wind. That person should not expect to receive anything from the Lord." And in Matthew 21:22, Jesus told His followers, "If you believe, you will receive whatever you ask for in prayer." So trust God's promise to help you! Even if your relationship with your daughter is rocky at times, trust that God is helping you know how to respond to her so that there is a long-term positive impact.

3. We Must Act on It

First John 5:15 says this about our prayers: "If we know that he hears us—whatever we ask—*we know that we have what we asked of him*." Don't sit around waiting for God to answer. Trust He has given you all the wisdom you need for a given situation, and then move forward in faith. Hebrews 11:1 says, "Now faith is confidence in what we hope for and assurance about what we do not see." If God promises He will give when you ask, then be assured of it and move forward.

With a constant awareness of our ability to not only influence our daughters but actually *inspire* them, we can move forward with a confidence that God will give us all we need to be the wind beneath their wings, their biggest fan, and their greatest inspiration.

A Look at Who You Are

1. Review the statements you wrote on page 24 about how you were influenced by your mom. If possible, contact your mother through an email, a letter, or a nice card and tell her what you appreciate about the positive qualities you inherited or learned from her. As you bless her, know that God has a way of bringing that blessing around to you later.

2. If you are still struggling with who you are today as a person and a mom—because of how you were raised, or because of any mistakes you have made in the past—write your name on the blanks below:

   "Therefore, if _____ is in Christ,
   _____ is a new creation; old things [about
   _____] have passed away; behold, all
   things have become new" (2 Corinthians 5:17 NKJV).

   That is your encouragement from God's Word if you are trusting in Christ alone for your salvation and depending on Him for the wisdom and strength you need to succeed in life.

3. Reflect on the fact that God knew all about you and yet He still decided you would be the best mom for your daughter. Write a short prayer of thanks to Him in the space below.

A Loving Look at Your Daughter

1. If possible, ask your daughter to fill out the following statements:

   My mother is very good at:

   My mother taught me to:

2. If she's willing, have your daughter make lists of the ways she is like
   and unlike you (as Dana did on page 28). If she doesn't live with you,
   ask her to email the lists. Trust me, you'll both have fun with this.
   Whether or not she writes her lists, you can fill out the lists below
   about the two of you:

Ways My Daughter Is Like Me:	Ways She Is Different from Me:

Now, look over your lists (or compare your lists with your daughter's)
and reflect. And when your heart is quiet and contemplative, offer the
following prayer on behalf of your daughter.

A Prayer for God's Help

Thank You, Lord, for giving me the privilege of being my daughter's mother. Thank You for the ways in which my daughter is like me. And thank You, too, for the ways she is unlike me. You have created her uniquely and I praise You for the young woman she is. Forgive me for expecting her to be like me in the ways that she is not. And help us to laugh and rejoice at the ways we are alike, as well as the ways that we are different.

Please, Father, give me wisdom and insight into how I can inspire her and encourage her in ways that are meaningful to her at this time in her life. And thank You that You desire the best for her even more than I do. I trust in the fact that, as much as I feel I don't get it right at times, You have appointed me to be the single most influential person in her life. May I hold that privilege and responsibility with great care, knowing You will equip me to do all that You have called me to do as her mother.

Chapter 2

Knowing What She Needs

Trust GOD from the bottom of your heart;
don't try to figure out everything on your own.
Listen for GOD's voice in everything you do, everywhere you go;
he's the one who will keep you on track.

PROVERBS 3:5-6 MSG

As a teenager, there were days when Shea put on the exterior that she didn't need a mother. Hurting because of difficult situations in her life, she took on the outer shell of a tough girl. But deep inside, she still needed her mother's love.

"Now that I am an adult, I see now that I needed discipline in a loving way from my mother. My parents divorced just before I entered the teen years, and my father was a bitter, angry, vengeful person. He often used my brother and me as pawns to anger or hurt my mother, so I found myself turning into a rebellious teen, full of anger and yet with a need to feel total and unconditional love. I distinctly remember there were moments I wished my mother would just hold me, let me cry, and tell me she loved me and everything would be okay.

"My mother did the best she could, and believe me, I really gave her a challenge. Even back then, I remember coming to the realization that although I continued to hurt my mother, and be disrespectful and manipulative, she loved me. She made it very clear that I was not walking with God and she did not approve of my attitude or actions, but she still loved me. Even when I could tell she didn't like me very much, I knew she loved me.

"As much as I say I needed comfort from her, we didn't grow up in an environment where that took place, and even if that wasn't the case I don't think I ever would have been open to it. I was a very closed-off young girl for a while."

But despite how Shea felt as a teenager, she says this today as a 27-year-old mother:

"My mother has truly been a rock through my storms in life. In July 2012, I prematurely gave birth to my first child via C-section, and was wheeled in for emergency open-heart surgery just 24 hours later to remove a tumor in my heart that was discovered soon after I had my son, Adyn. Even though it had been nearly 30 years since my mother had raised a baby, she stepped up to care for my son when I physically couldn't. While I was in the hospital recovering, she made sure my husband and I had everything we needed, and she sat with the baby until he was ready to go home from the hospital. Without blinking an eye, she got my son on a routine—including feedings and getting him to the first doctor's appointment.

"I am still recovering from the surgeries, but I am surrounded by help, and my son is surrounded with love. There were times when I physically could not hold or console him, and my mom was there. She has shown her immense love for me by giving more than I could ever ask for. She has welcomed us to stay with her while I go through rehab, get back to work, and try to take care of the financial responsibilities coming our way. Her faith-filled life, strength (which she will say only comes from God—I don't think she gives herself enough credit), and unconditional love have left big shoes for me to fill."

What was most important to Shea? That fact that her mother was there when she needed her. That cemented a bond between the two of them.

She Feels My Pain

Kristen, age 20, sings similar praises about her mother, whom she calls "the most amazing woman in the world."

"My mother came through for me in a huge way. Last year, I shattered my vertebrae to complete dust in a very terrible accident. She did not leave my side for one second. She stayed up for days on end during my surgery. She is the only one who feels my pain when I am in pain. Because of her countless acts of selfless and undying love for me, I was able to walk again and make an almost complete recovery. My mother held my hand when I lay there dying and helped me to hold on. I don't know what I, or my family, would do without her. She is my rock, my inspiration, and my hope."

She Has My Back

And Annemarie Gregory, 21, says this about what she needed in a mom:

"I needed to know my mom was on my side. She was always loving and hardworking, and she listened well, but at the end of the day I needed to know she understood. Even if she didn't necessarily agree or know what to say, I needed to know she 'had my back.' I desperately needed to know she was with me—that no matter what boy had broken my heart, how frustrating a math problem was, or that I had failed to do the dishes, she was in my corner. Besides, she was—and still is!—a force to be reckoned with. It's great to have her in my corner!"

Could it be said any clearer? A daughter needs her mother's love and support—her time, her presence, her heart. In fact, more than what you *do*, she needs *you*.

Guesswork Mothering

Wouldn't it be wonderful if our daughters came out of the womb telling us in very clear language exactly what they needed? Yet so often we guess at it, make the mistakes, and then see clearly in hindsight what we should have done. Many times as a mom you may focus on what you think is important to your daughter, only to find out later all she really wanted and needed was *you*. Your time. Your presence. Your heart.

There seems to be so much guesswork when it comes to mothering a daughter, especially during the teen years, but there doesn't need to be. Shea's, Kristen's, and Annemarie's moms were just being mom to their daughters—being there for them when they needed it. Sounds simple, yet giving of ourselves is sometimes the hardest thing for us to do.

What Your Daughter Needs

As I surveyed daughters between the ages of 15 and 40, I discovered what they wanted most from their mothers. I found that what they didn't need was more money, more leniency when it comes to the household rules, a nicer home, a private school, or more opportunities for extracurricular involvement. Surprisingly, *none* of those things were mentioned at all. Instead, what they *all* said they needed—and still need—is their mother's "love and support."

In fact, that phrase "love and support" was mentioned first on nearly every survey and in nearly every interview I conducted, regardless of the woman's age, ethnicity, religious background, or economic status.

My daughter, Dana, now 21, says, "I needed my mother's love and support in everything I did. Even when I did something completely wrong, I needed her to love me anyway and to let me know things were going to be okay."

So what does "love and support" look like?

She Needs to Know She Is Your Priority

As a 19-year-old college student who has never doubted her mother's love for her, Annie says, "My mom made me her center. I don't think that spoiled me. Rather, it made me secure in the fact that she loved me and would do what it took to provide for all I needed."

Dana said, "Not to sound selfish, but I needed my mom to choose me first over a lot of things, to let me know that I was a priority in her life over work and finances."

The one thing we so often feel we don't have is often the one thing our daughters would rather have than anything else: our time. A daughter's need for her mother's time, prioritization, and involvement in her life is so huge that I've dedicated a couple chapters to this. So we will come back to this matter in chapters 4 and 5 and explore ways you can prioritize your daughter and become interested in and involved in her world.

She Needs Your Acceptance

Nearly every woman whom I interviewed for this book indicated she needed acceptance from her mom, regardless of her age. She needed to feel accepted as she was recognizing her uniqueness, in the ways she felt "odd" or out of place in a crowd, and on the days she felt she didn't measure up to others around her. As I look back on my own childhood, I remember I felt a strong need for acceptance, too, in light of growing up next to an older sister whom I felt was much more accomplished that I was. With that in mind, in chapter 3 we will look at ways you can build up your daughter, encourage her heart, and help her to feel accepted.

She Needs to Feel a Connection with You

Karen said she never really felt a solid emotional connection with her mom.

"My mom was a single parent raising me and my siblings. She worked outside of the home through most of my adolescent years. I didn't feel a connection with her because she had a 'hard shell' around her heart. While I always knew she loved me, it was very difficult to approach her.

"Even as I matured and became a wife and mother, I did not feel I could share with her the secret places of my heart. I never really felt like I could talk intimately with her. Only a few times can I remember opening up and sharing deep thoughts with her." We will look later at how Karen became the kind of mother to her own daughter that she wished she had as a child.

She Needs a Spiritual Foundation

Katie, who was raised in a strong Christian home, says that although she might not have appreciated it at the time, her mother's insistence that she attend church every Sunday and learn biblical values was one of the best things her mother could've done for her. Katie intends to do this as well with her own children.

Krystle, who is raising a teen and preteen daughter, said she wishes her mom had made more of an effort to bring her up spiritually.

"My mother was a loving, devoted, Christian stay-at-home mom up until my parents divorced when I was around seven years old. Our lifestyle changed dramatically after that. My mother struggled to support and raise four children on her own. She became discouraged and left her church for a while. She worked a lot, and turned to friends and partying. She became more focused on her life and her needs and didn't encourage her children enough. I feel that my mom should have drawn closer to the Lord during those days."

Our daughters need us to have a strong dependence on the Lord so they can imitate that and develop a dependence on the Lord as well. In chapter 9, we will look at how to provide spiritual guidance to our daughters.

She Needs to Be Allowed to Fail

One young woman who was raised with a strong spiritual foundation said she wishes her parents had realized she was human and she would indeed fail.

"I felt fortunate that both my parents were great examples who showed love to me all the time. The downside for me was that I never felt I could be completely open and honest because the lines between right and wrong were so clearly drawn I was afraid I wouldn't be accepted when I made mistakes. I wish I had been given permission to make mistakes without danger of judgment. That's not to say I would have made better choices than I already did, but when I messed up, I felt as though my mom wasn't approachable."

When our daughters are young, there are times when we want to step in and do something for them rather than risk their becoming disappointed or having to watch them fail. But it is crucial to their development as young women to learn how to pick themselves up after they fail and move on. Your daughter needs to be okay with the fact that it's perfectly normal and human to make mistakes. She needs to know it isn't the end of the world if she fails to do something right. And she needs to know that coming in second or third—or not placing at all—is often a part of life.

Being allowed to fail—or even make a mistake—was not something that Kelly experienced while growing up.

"I needed my mom to show me that imperfection was not failure," Kelly says. "I needed her to show me what real failure was."

Kelly explains: "I was very hard on myself if I didn't do something perfectly, even on the first try. This weighed on me immensely. I developed low self-esteem because I felt I wasn't good or worthy. I needed my mom to show me that my imperfection was normal. She never did. She never addressed it. She saw me being crushed and she never once tried to help. She could have at least tried to see what was causing the strain. It took years of God's grace and loving friends to help me understand that imperfection was normal and acceptable."

Guiding your daughter through disappointment and failure is just as important as guiding her through victory and success. Let her make mistakes. Let her feel badly. Let her live out what it's like to be imperfect. And love her through it all. In doing so, you show her very tangibly the way God loves her.

She Needs You to Be a Woman of Integrity

When my husband, Hugh, was in Bible college studying to be a pastor, he met J.I. Packer, a Bible scholar, author, and veteran pastor. Hugh asked him: "What is the most important thing for me to focus on in my quest to become a pastor?" Packer's response was packed with wisdom. He looked at Hugh straight in the eyes, and said, firmly but gently, "Your own personal holiness. That is your congregation's greatest need."

I can't help but think that is my daughter's greatest need from me as well. I can raise her according to biblical principles, give her a foundation of biblical instruction, talk to her about the importance of being Christlike and loving others and having a pure heart. But the bottom line is that if I'm not modeling any of it myself, then my words are merely words. Dana needs to see my personal holiness if she is to become a woman who desires holiness as well. She needs to see it lived out in me every day of my life and know it is real before she will know how or even have a desire to live it herself. She needs an example to follow when it comes to making life's choices and being the woman she knows I want her to be.

She Needs Your Stability—and Your Discernment

Notice I didn't say your daughter needs her *own* stability. That's because I believe your daughter will be as emotionally stable as you are. One 19-year-old daughter told me, "I wish I could be real with my mom, but I can't show anything she might perceive as weakness because she'll feel guilty or feel my insecurity or hardship is her fault. She carries a lot of guilt and burdens on her shoulders."

Your daughter needs you to be a woman who lays her burdens at God's feet. Then she won't feel as though your burdens are piling up on her shoulders instead.

She also needs you to be a woman of discernment no matter how old she is, no matter how old *you* are. Knowing what to say—as well as what *not* to say—is important for your daughter. KJ, now 33, expressed frustration over the way her mom said *too much* about her personal and marital struggles.

"I wish my mom hadn't shared so much about the troubles in her own marriage. I didn't and still don't know how to handle and process that information. Whose side do I take? *Should* I take sides? How do I tell my mom that she is wrong and the Christlike thing to do is to love my dad and let God deal with their problems?" KJ wasn't talking about anything that endangered her mother. Instead, she was talking about the way her mom expressed frustration over her father's drinking and buying lottery tickets. Like any child, KJ felt—and still feels—unsure of how to respond when her mother shares such information with her.

Another daughter, now in college, expressed similar feelings: "My mom 'threw up' on me at times—telling me in great detail how she felt about what was going on with her and my dad. She really should have kept some things more private. She was way too embarrassed to talk to her friends, so she would talk to me." The result of that lack of discernment on her mother's part? "I often had to act as her counselor," this frustrated daughter said. "Even up to last year, I was trying to be their marriage counselor because she put me in that position."

Your daughter needs *you* to be the parent. You can get needy with your girlfriends, but not with your daughter. Don't cross the line of making her feel uncomfortable. One daughter said, "My mom allowed me to 'parent' her. There were times I had to take care of her emotionally when I needed it to be the other way around."

Our daughters can't carry us emotionally. That is a load they weren't intended to bear. Nor can they heal us of our insecurities or fill the various voids in our lives. Only God can bind up our deepest wounds (Psalm 147:3).[7]

Are there issues in your life that are preventing you from having a healthy relationship with your daughter? Are *you* a woman who feels loved, supported, accepted, and secure, or are you trying to feel that way through your relationship with your daughter? Again, if you did not receive these things from your mother, you have a heavenly Father who can more than make up for what you lacked. It is His regenerative work in your life that makes you able to be the parent for your daughter that you always wanted but perhaps never had. Trust the work He is wanting to do in you, and you may see it spill over into your daughter's life as well.

So Now What?

You may be naturally hard on yourself as you evaluate what kind of mother you are, or what kind of mom you've been to your daughter thus far. But please know that our daughters aren't as hard on us as we are on ourselves. In fact, as I surveyed many daughters aged 18 through 30, I was pleasantly surprised to find that most were far more gracious, forgiving, and positive toward their mothers than their mothers were toward themselves or their own moms. Could this be that the younger generation of women is more forgiving and less critical of us than we are of ourselves? If yes, praise God for that! And may it give you hope to know that your daughter probably sees you through much softer lenses than you see yourself.

Know What Speaks Love to Her

Sometimes we make the mistake of assuming that things of importance to us are equally important to our daughters. And we think the things that aren't a big deal to us also aren't a big deal to them. But when Dana was a young teenager, my mom told me I'd be surprised at what Dana will remember as being significant or what she will brush off as being minor. Sure enough, there are things Dana remembers as especially wonderful that I don't even remember doing.

What is important to you may not be as important to your daughter. Likewise, what is very important to her might not seem at all significant to you. That's why it's crucial for you to know what speaks love to her and what doesn't.

A Look at What *You* Needed

Sometimes the best indicator of what your daughter needs from you is to look back and remember what you needed most from your own mother.

As I interviewed women for this book, I saw a lot of mother-daughter wounds surface. I gained a lot of insight about how a woman's relationship with her mother greatly impacts how she parents her daughter. I found that some moms who had nothing but wonderful things to say about their relationship with their own moms were experiencing similarly good relationships with their daughters. Other moms, however, had difficult or hurtful relationships with their moms, and were experiencing similar difficulties as they related to their daughters.

"My mom wasn't a good role model when it came to being a parent," one middle-aged mom told me. It is unfortunate when that happens, but it doesn't have to determine our destiny. It can, instead, be our motivator to be the best role model our daughter will ever have.

When I was a young teenager, my mother told me that "we can learn from the opposites." We can see what we don't want to imitate and allow it to be our motivation to do things differently. The fact that we lack something—physically, emotionally, or spiritually—in our own upbringing can serve as a powerful motivator to make sure our own children don't experience that same lack.

Giving Her What You Never Had

Sometimes we moms shy away from giving our daughters what we ourselves never had. We don't necessarily do this on purpose. We just tend to mother them in the way that we were mothered. But if there was something lacking in your life as you grew up, take the opportunity now, with your daughter, to give what you never had.

Denise is an example of a mother who did just that. Denise grew up in the 1970s—a generation during which moms didn't do a lot of snuggling with their kids. They were busy working at jobs, doing laundry, cooking meals (before the era of fast food and microwaves), and more. Even as stay-at-home moms, they were busy. So Denise, the oldest of three children, often wondered if she was loved. "I know now my mom was just doing what she knew to do," Denise said. But when she had her own daughter,

Brooke, Denise poured on the affection so her daughter would never feel that same insecurity.

Today, Brooke is the mother of two small children. And she knows she is loved.

"My mom snuggled us. A lot. Likewise, I insist on showing my children physical affection. My husband did not come from a home with a lot of hugging and kissing, but to me that's how you show love. I always knew my mom loved me—without a doubt. And the affection had a lot to do with that."

Denise drew from what she had wanted (not necessarily what she had experienced) and started a new legacy of showing love and affection in her family. And her daughter, Brooke, is continuing that legacy of being a family that snuggles, cuddles, and is warmly affectionate with each other.

You can begin a new legacy too.

Shea, the 27-year-old whose story started this chapter, says now that she is a mother of a toddler, she understands how her mom gave from an area in which she had lacked as a child.

"My mom grew up in a home where 'I love you' just wasn't said, so she made sure that us kids heard it a lot. We can never say we weren't sure our mom loved us. She *made sure* we knew it."

And Karen, who never felt a close emotional connection with her mother, made sure she was open, honest, and approachable with her own daughter so she would never have to feel that lack in their relationship.

Karen's daughter is now 20 years old. "We have a close and loving relationship and even talk about intimate topics," Karen says. "She has shared important emotional situations with me and trusts that I will keep these subjects private. Now that she is in a dating relationship with a young man at her college, I have to respect her and not probe too deeply about her new boyfriend. The fact that I wait and allow her to approach me with details about their relationship makes it very special when she does share something with me that is personal."

I know many women who lacked a spiritual foundation as they grew up, and they've made that their first priority in raising their own daughter. Or, they married unbelievers and had no idea how much they would struggle in their marriage relationship because of it, so they are determined to train their daughters in the importance of God's command to not marry an unbeliever.[8] These moms are giving their daughters the instruction or experiences they never received from their own moms.

That's why it's so important for us to look at what we are doing as moms. We can very easily repeat the same dysfunctional patterns we grew up with without even realizing it. So we need to be deliberate and intentional about what we want to change or do differently when it comes to mothering our own children.

Starting a New Legacy

Every girl goes through certain experiences while growing up that she doesn't want repeated in her own marriage and family. When I was growing up, my parents experienced a rocky marriage that ended in divorce when I was 19 years old. During the difficult year that they divorced, my prayer was, "God, teach me what *not* to do through what I am seeing right now. Help me to not imitate any unhealthy behavior that I've been exposed to." And yet there are days when shadows of my past seem to linger large and I start to feel defeated, as if I have no choice but to repeat some of the baggage from my past. It is then that I must apply the truth of God's Word to my life and let it shine through any darkness that might still linger from my past.

Second Corinthians 5:17 says, "If anyone is in Christ, [she] is a new creature; the old things passed away; behold, new things have come" (NASB). That verse means I am not destined to repeat the patterns of the past, and neither are you. I also receive hope from 2 Corinthians 1:3-4, which reminds me that I can be strengthened and empowered through some of the difficult situations I've faced in my past. In that passage I find a principle that has guided me through all types of hurt in my life:

> Praise be to the God and Father of our Lord Jesus Christ, the Father of compassion and the God of all comfort, who comforts us in all our troubles, so that we can comfort those in any trouble with the comfort we ourselves receive from God.

Did your parents experience a rocky marriage that left you feeling insecure? Maybe you haven't realized this up to now, but God can use your past experiences to inspire you to provide stability and security for your daughter, especially if she has witnessed you in a rocky marriage as well. Did you lack affection from your mom while growing up? Maybe you haven't realized it, but God's heart was there for you, giving you comfort in spite of your lack. As you reflect on how God has come through for you or you realize God's love and comfort for you, can you in turn offer that to your daughter? God won't waste a wound. And He can make you stronger through your wound so that you become a more loving mother, rather than the opposite.

You see, regardless of what you have experienced, God is the perfect parent. He has expressed perfect, unconditional love toward you, and He can help you love your daughter with not just a mother's love, but with His perfect love.

God Modeled It for Us

In the Bible we have a beautiful description of what God's perfect love looks like:

> Love is patient, love is kind and is not jealous; love does not brag and is not arrogant, does not act unbecomingly; it does not seek its own, is not provoked, does not take into account a wrong suffered, does not rejoice in unrighteousness, but rejoices with the truth; bears all things, believes all things, hopes all things, endures all things. Love never fails (1 Corinthians 13:4-8 NASB).

I remember being told, when I was in high school, to read those verses and substitute my name where the word "love" appeared to see how accurate of a description that passage was (or was not) of me. This was a great exercise for convicting me of how I wasn't loving others the way I should. But the older I get, and the more I understand the love and grace of God, the more I believe that portion of Scripture is not there solely to *convict* us of what we *should* be doing, but also to *comfort* us (and motivate us) with a good look at the kind of love that God has bestowed on us. First Corinthians 13:4-8 is a description of God's love toward us. We are told in 1 John 4 that "God is love" (verses 8,16). So look at 1 Corinthians 13:4-8 again, this time with *God's* name, not yours, substituted for the word "love," and drink in its meaning:

> [God] is patient, [God] is kind and is not jealous; [God] does not brag and is not arrogant, does not act unbecomingly; ... does not seek [His] own, is not provoked, does not take into account a wrong suffered, does not rejoice in unrighteousness, but rejoices with the truth; [God] bears all things, believes all things, hopes all things, endures all things. [God] never fails.

That is the kind of love that God, as your heavenly Father, shows you. Can you parent your daughter with the same love? Of course you can—through God's help. Through God loving your daughter through you. If you had a mother who showed you that kind of love, doing this will be easier for you. But if not, God can more than make up for what you lacked from a loving mother through the unconditional, ever-present love He has shown toward you. When you begin to love your daughter as God loves you, you are truly giving her the "love and support" she needs—

- regardless of what she's done,
- regardless of how long it's been since she's talked with you,
- regardless of whether she is living or acting the way you would prefer,
- regardless of your feelings for her on any given day.

You Were Chosen for This Task

I mentioned at the beginning of this book that you are not your daughter's mother by accident. You were chosen and appointed by God. And that means God must have known you were up to the task, or that the task would compel you to kneel down in surrender at His feet. It is God's intention to make you like Himself in every way, so He will use whatever it takes—maybe even parenting your daughter—to bring you to a place of surrender and Christlikeness. So, my friend, gain confidence in the fact that where God guides, He provides. As He calls you, He will equip you. As you call upon Him for help, He will welcome you with open arms.

God knows what your daughter needs even more than you do. And He can help you be the mother He specifically designed you to be.

Ephesians 2:10 says we are "God's handiwork, created in Christ Jesus to do good works, which God prepared in advance for us to do." That means when God created you, He created you to not only be His servant, but to do good works (like mothering), which He prepared in advance for you to do. God designated, before time began, that you would not only be a mother, but whose mother you would be. He was fully aware of your personality and your abilities and your limitations, as well as those of your daughter. And in His perfect design, He still gave her to you and you to her.

So rest in that, dear mom. The One who has entrusted you with this task has not abandoned you, nor will He ever (Hebrews 13:5). He is at your side, ready to help at any moment that you call.

························· From Her Perspective ·························

"What I Thought I Needed..."

Christen, a 23-year-old college graduate, reflected on what she felt she needed from her mom when she was younger and what she now realizes she needed all along:

"What I *perceived* I needed and what I *really* needed were two different things. As a child, I thought I needed a mom who never made me do chores, who never got mad when I did something wrong, or who didn't make me play the piano. But as a grown woman, I now realize that all that is *exactly* what I needed. I needed a mother who taught me to work hard, who taught me the consequences of my actions, and who taught me that hard work pays off in the end. I now also realize that my deepest need was for a faith in the Lord and Savior Jesus Christ. I needed a mother who taught me to pray when I lay down at night and arose in the morning. I needed a mother who modeled this faith through the harvests and the deserts of life.

"My mother did not fit into my childish expectations of what I needed. Rather, she overflowed the expectations of what I now realize I needed. Apart from what I previously mentioned, she also provided a nurturing and comforting spirit that helped to revive me after my choices and life experiences left me broken by pain and betrayal. She has always done everything to go above and beyond what I believed I needed and provide a strength that I took for granted."

Don't underestimate, dear mom, the value of the love and labor you have invested thus far in your daughter's life. And don't think that if you haven't given her as much as you had hoped that it's too late for her to want and appreciate it now. Just as she will always be your "little girl," you will always be her mom. And more than anything else, more than anyone else, your daughter needs *you*.

A Look at What She Needs

1. Which of the following needs are you finding it a challenge for you to meet right now for your daughter? Circle the ones you need to commit to prayer:

   Prioritizing her

   Accepting her

   Connecting with her

   Providing a spiritual foundation for her

   Allowing her to fail

   Being a woman of integrity

   Your own stability/discernment

2. If your daughter is 12 years old or older, ask her, in a kind and loving way, "What is the one thing you need the most from me at this point in your life?" Her answer may open your eyes to needs you haven't paid enough attention to. Once she tells you, thank her for her honesty and commit those needs to prayer, asking God for the wisdom and discernment to meet your daughter's needs in practical ways.

Praying for What She Needs

God, I need Your wisdom for discerning how to meet
my daughter's needs. I want to show her my love and
support in every way possible, but it is so easy for me to
be remiss and to let something slip through the cracks.
Give me insightful eyes and a listening ear to recognize
when she needs a hug, an encouraging word, or some
of my time. Impress upon my heart how I can be there
for her in the ways she needs me most.

Chapter 3

Building Her Up

Some people make cutting remarks,
but the words of the wise bring healing.

PROVERBS 12:18 NLT

Chelsea is one of the most confident young women I know. Straight out of college, she landed her first job at a Christian high school where she teaches drama, public speaking, choir, and Bible. She has a beautiful smile, a contagious enthusiasm, and a passion for God. But Chelsea didn't get where she is today by accident. Chelsea had a mom who knew how to build her up and encourage her heart all through her growing-up years.

"My mom has always been my biggest fan and has encouraged me to pursue excellence in everything," Chelsea said. "She and I are best friends and I think a lot of that has to do with the fact that she was willing to listen when I shared my struggles with her as I was becoming a young woman.

"When I was in seventh grade, my nickname was 'Cherry-face Chelsea' because my face was always red. I thought of myself as ugly because I compared myself to the girls who had dark hair and were well tanned," she said.

"Then my mom told me of all the beautiful actresses who had fair skin and that most models are fair as well. She also explained that because my skin was porcelain, I wouldn't wrinkle or suffer from sun damage someday. She told me about all the things that I have that others don't, like pretty rosy cheeks that don't need blush and bright blond hair that will turn a pretty white when I'm older, not a dirty gray. She also told me that the things I was worried about would not be all that important to me when I grew older. She helped me see that in the scope of my life, it was very minimal that kids teased me for having a red face. She said having friends, getting good grades, being nice to others, and being liked by nearly everyone was what was truly important, not the trivial things the world says are popular."

As Chelsea grew older, her mom continued to build her up and encourage her.

"She always pushed me to be excellent, never let me give up, and always told me that a godly woman sticks to her commitments and gives a million percent even when she doesn't want to."

One summer, Chelsea was hired as the assistant program director at a camp in the mountains. It was a four-month-long job and Chelsea wasn't faring well out in nature with insects and the lack of conveniences that she had access to at home.

"I had a break the third weekend and went home and told my mom that I hated it and didn't want to go back," Chelsea said. "But she told me that I needed to stick to the commitment that I had made, and she encouraged me to find even the slightest bit of joy in the little things during the day to keep me going. I went back to the camp and started to look for the little things that would keep my spirits up. My mom also suggested that I see if there was a way I could use my music skills at the camp because she knew my passion for music. When I went back, I talked to the camp director and we checked all the upcoming camps to see if they had a worship leader. If they didn't, I would serve as the worship leader, which was something I never would have thought of myself.

"I also believe that a lot of my drive to become a successful young woman stemmed from the fact that my mom always cared about every detail of my life. Even if I came home from school with the most ridiculously unimportant story to tell her, she would make me feel like it was somehow the greatest thing she'd heard all day. Just knowing she cared pushed me toward excellence because I didn't want to let her down. And if I ever did let her down, she never made me feel horrible for it. She would encourage me to do better the next time around, and she pointed out good lessons to be learned from the mistakes I made."

The Value of Your Words

Perhaps your daughter doesn't struggle with feeling that she's ugly. Maybe, instead, she struggles with fear—fear that she will make a mistake, let you down, or fail to make the grade. Perhaps she is shy and withdrawn. Maybe she struggles in school and therefore doesn't believe she's capable of much. Or, maybe she has a history of giving up, or a hesitancy to commit to something or trust someone. Or, it's possible she has had all your time, love, and support and *still* feels she needs more.

Regardless of your daughter's age, regardless of how easy or difficult her life is at this point, regardless of how independent she may appear, she still needs her mother's encouragement. She needs to be built up by the woman closest to her.

While writing my book *When a Woman Overcomes Life's Hurts*, I found that among the deepest wounds in a woman's life are the words of a critical mother, or a mom who was absent or uninvolved in her daughter's life.

"She never told me she was proud of me," "I never felt like I had her approval," or "I never felt I was good enough in her eyes" were some of the most common wounds expressed among women, regardless of their age.

It's so very easy for us as moms to be critical—especially if we grew up hearing more criticism than praise from our own moms. But we can change that pattern and become moms who build up our daughters and encourage their hearts. Everyone loves to hear encouragement. And when we become women who build up others, including our daughters, they will want us around all of their lives.

So what are some ways you can lift up your daughter so she can bloom to her full potential?

Christi, who had an encouraging mother and strives to be that kind of mom to her teenage daughter, listed ways that she has encouraged Alexis, who is now 15:

- When she was young, I listed all the people who loved her (and I made the list long, and punctuated it with God and Jesus).

- I said "I love you *this* much," and I would throw my arms open as wide as possible.

- I constantly told her, and continue to tell her, that she can do anything she aspires to. (We often dream together of what her future life will be like.)
- I hug her in the morning and say, "I love you" and I hug her again before bed at night with another "I love you."

Tame Your Tongue

To build up your daughter, you must know what to say as well as what not to say. James 3:5-8 tells us that even though the tongue is one of the smallest parts of our bodies, it can do much damage. That passage also calls the tongue "a fire" and tells us "no man can tame the tongue. It is a restless evil, full of deadly poison" (verse 8).

Because "no man [or woman] can tame the tongue," we need *God's* help to control what we say and how we say it, lest we burn others, our daughters included, with what we say.

How many times have we let slip a hurtful word and then wished we had kept it at bay? How many times have we spoken something out of turn or that wasn't true, and seen a forest fire spread? Hopefully those are lessons we learned when we were young so we aren't still making those mistakes today...especially with our daughters. We can do much damage with our tongues if we are not asking God to tame them.

Build Her Up Through Words

Because the tongue can be so very powerful, we must learn to use it constructively to not tear down or burn up, but to positively train and build up. Ephesians 4:29 tells us:

> Let no unwholesome word proceed from your mouth, but only such a word as is good for edification according to the need of the moment, so that it will give grace to those who hear (NASB).

In the New International Version, that verse reads:

> Do not let any unwholesome talk come out of your mouths, but only what is helpful for building others up according to their needs, that it may benefit those who listen.

Now, let's take that verse apart and look at five principles for building up others—and specifically, our daughters—with our words.

Principle #1: Keep it clean—*"Let no unwholesome word…"*

Our daughters will talk how we talk. They will imitate our tone, our choice of words, and even our sounds, such as sighs, grunts, and eye rolls, which can say more than a thousand words! Sometimes an unwholesome word is something negative said about someone else. A critical comment or a harsh word that hurts (even if it's not directed at our daughters) is unscriptural and a poor example of love and encouragement.

Principle #2: Keep it in—*"Let no unwholesome word proceed from your mouth…"*

Here's the rub, moms. Many words form instantly in our minds, but will we let them escape our lips? Oh, how I wish there were some words I'd never said. Words said in anger, frustration, or pain that roll out uncontrolled can be the most damaging. James 1:19 says, "Everyone should be quick to listen, slow to speak and slow to become angry." Remembering that verse might help you keep unwholesome words from coming out of your mouth. It has helped me on a number of occasions.

Principle #3: Keep it positive—*"but only such a word as is good for edification…"*

Oh, the power of the word "only." What if the *only* words we let proceed out of our mouths were words that built others up? The beauty of that verse is that we can correct by building up. We can counsel by building up. We can exhort, reprove, and train by building up. We can even discipline by building up. To build up our daughter in everything we say doesn't mean we turn into a softie. It means we build her into the woman she was designed to be with words that will help and guide her at the proper time.

Principle #4: Keep it timely—*"according to the need of the moment…"*

Sometimes the best word is no word at all. At other times, only praise is necessary. Sometimes what your daughter needs most is understanding, not a lecture. Or she may need a simple "I'm sorry" when she's lost a competition or a job or a boyfriend rather than advice on what she could've or should've done better. Proverbs 15:23 says, "A person finds joy in giving an apt reply—and how good is a timely word!"

Principle #5: Keep it gracious—*"that it will give grace to those who hear."*

How do you give grace to your daughter through your words? By giving her understanding when she deserved a lecture. By saying kind words when she doesn't necessarily deserve them. God extended grace toward His people when He said, "I have loved you with an everlasting love" (Jeremiah 31:3) and "For God so loved the world..." (John 3:16). Those words, spoken to a people who didn't deserve them (and none of us do), are now treasured by those of us who believe them. Speak words that your daughter will treasure.

Looking once again at Ephesians 4:29, let's see how it appears in The Message:

> Watch the way you talk. Let nothing foul or dirty come out of your mouth. Say only what helps, each word a gift.

The Gift of Words

Imagine if each word you gave to your daughter was a gift—a timely, treasured gift that built her up and showed her grace.

Sarah Tipton shared a story with me of edifying words, spoken from her dying mother, at precisely the time she needed to hear them. They were words that became a treasured, timely gift:

"Mom was dying of colon cancer. I was at her bedside in the hospital with my 2½-month-old daughter.

"'Mom,' I asked her, 'Do you think I will be a good mom?'

"I can still hear her answer: 'Sarah, I *know* you will be a good mom.'

"What a blessing it has been to carry that with me through the years."

Sarah's mom, before dying, could have listed suggestions or important values or uncompromising principles that her daughter should reflect on and implement as a new mom. She could have talked of the things she did well or the things she regretted doing herself. She could have used that time to apologize or make it all about herself. But instead, she built up her daughter with a few choice words that were soothing to Sarah's soul. "Sarah, I *know* you will be a good mom."

What words does your daughter need to hear from you? Chances are she needs to hear that you are proud of her, that you believe in her, and that she is beautiful.

Say You're Proud of Her

I don't believe Dana has ever (nor will ever) lose the desire for her mother's approval and praise. She obviously has the love language of affirmation and encouraging words. From the time she was young she would immediately ask me, after a performance, "Did you like my song?" or "Did you see my dance? What did you think?" or just a "How did I do?" Even if everyone else in the room said she did a great job, she still needed to hear it from me. Of course she did! I'm her mom. Today, when she performs a solo beautifully or tries something new on the piano, even though she does it with confidence and ease, she will come back to her seat, search the auditorium for my eyes, and give me that look that asks (or she'll actually mouth the words), "How did I do?" I love that she still cares what I think. And it is now my goal to praise her *before* she has a chance to ask. I know that means a lot to her.

Even if your daughter has heard it a thousand times, know that no matter how many people tell her she did a great job, she will still need to hear it from her mom. Yes, girls go through that age—usually in their teen years—when they act like they don't want to hear it, or they blush or roll their eyes (especially when a comment comes from their mothers). But don't let that fool you. Your words carry more weight than most everyone else's. Tell her you are proud of her. And tell her often.

Show Her You Believe in Her

You can tell your daughter you believe in her. But your actions will always speak louder than your words. To show her you believe in her and her abilities, as well as her hopes and dreams, come alongside her and help her in a tangible way.

My friend Chris, who maintains a close relationship with her stepdaughter, Cristina, says, "I built her up with words. I still try to. There were definitely times I tore her down with just a look and I definitely regret that today. But there were more times that I built her up by coming alongside her and helping her with those things I was initially critical of. And I prayed for her continually, and still do."

Cristina says that's the one action of her stepmom's that has impacted her the most: "She comes alongside me in areas where I need help and that's what really inspires me to do more, go beyond myself, minister to others, and try new things."

Tell Her She's Beautiful

Your daughter also needs to hear from you that she's beautiful. I remember my mom telling me that whenever she asked her mom if she was pretty, her mom would say, "You're pretty when you smile," or "What's important is that you are pretty on the inside." And while her mom was trying to impart a spiritual truth about inner beauty, my mom still wondered, while growing up, if she was a pretty girl.

Judy says, "I felt my parents didn't give me quite enough confidence in myself. So with Sherry [her stepdaughter], I've tried to build up her confidence. I always told her how pretty and sweet she was. I constantly told her I'm proud of her, and I still do that today."

Sherry adds, "It never gets old, to hear that she's proud of me and to hear her affirming me."

Practice Saying *Whatever*

The word *whatever* can carry with it negative connotations. It has become a flippant "I really don't care" type of statement that we say when we are frustrated or feeling indifferent. But I want you to start seeing the word *whatever* as a guideline and filter for what you *should* say when it comes to talking to your daughter and building her up.

Philippians 4:8 spells out what our minds should think on by giving us a list of "whatevers." I like to apply this verse about our thoughts and extend it to how we should *speak* and what we should speak *about*, as well:

> Brothers and sisters, whatever is true, whatever is noble, whatever is right, whatever is pure, whatever is lovely, whatever is admirable—if anything is excellent or praiseworthy—think about such things.

If we talk to our daughter about only what is true, that will eliminate, gossip from our lips. If we talk only about what is noble, right, pure, lovely, and admirable, it will keep us from talking critically about anyone or mentioning anything that we shouldn't. We will be modeling Christlikeness to our daughters while building them up rather than tearing them—or others—down.

There are more "whatevers" in Scripture that can serve as further guidelines on how to hold our tongues, speak uprightly, and encourage our daughters:

Whatever you do—First Corinthians 10:31 tells us, "So whether you eat or drink or *whatever you do* [this would include whatever you say], do it all for the glory of God." In other words, our very lifestyle is to reflect God's glory, so everything we do—whether we speak or remain silent—should glorify God.

Whatever happens—Philippians 1:27 instructs, "*Whatever happens*, conduct yourselves in a manner worthy of the gospel of Christ." This means whatever your daughter does or says, whatever circumstance sends you over the edge, whatever is said to or about your daughter, we are to conduct ourselves worthy of the gospel of Christ. In other words, there is never a reason for us to "go off" verbally and destructively.

Whatever you say—Colossians 3:17 exhorts us in this way: "*Whatever you do, whether in word or deed,* do it all in the name of the Lord Jesus, giving thanks to God the Father through him." This verse is telling us to make sure every action we take and every word we speak is a good representation of Christ, and is done and said with a grateful heart. Wow, that doesn't leave much room for you and me to just "speak our minds" when we've had it, does it? Yet having a thankful mind-set and a determination to represent Christ well ensures that the words that come out of our mouths will be uplifting and healthy, rather than damaging and hurtful.

Build Her Up Through Prayer

The most effective way you can build up your daughter is through prayer. When Dana was in elementary school, I was a member of Moms in Prayer (formerly called Moms in Touch), and we would meet weekly to pray Scripture over our children's lives.[9] During those years I realized that far more could be accomplished by talking to God about Dana than by talking to Dana about God. If there were issues about her attitudes or her actions, God could work within her heart, through my prayers, much better than I could try to get into her heart and work things out on my own.

You may have a daughter who needs to be told, countless times, that she's beautiful or capable or talented, but she still may not believe it. You may have a daughter who is struggling with identity or confidence issues that you can't seem to penetrate. That's when you go to work on her heart through the power of prayer. That's when you change your tactic and, in addition to telling her what God thinks about her or how you love her or what she needs to do to be open to instruction, you ask God to impress upon her heart who she is in *His* eyes. (God already knows what your daughter needs, and He is able to penetrate her thoughts when you are unable to, or when she is incapable of hearing it from you at this time in her life.)

Pray for Discernment

Because our words can have such a strong impact on our daughters, it is so very important that we be wise and discerning when it comes to building them up and encouraging them. And where can we find that wisdom and discernment?

James 1:5 says, "If any of you lacks wisdom, you should ask God, who gives generously to all without finding fault, and it will be given to you." When it comes to wisdom for raising our daughters and knowing what they need, all we have to do is ask God for it. When we ask Him, He will give it to us *generously* and *without finding fault*.

Let's take a closer look at that verse, for it tells us *three* amazing things about the way God gives us wisdom.

1. He gives wisdom to us "generously"

In the original Greek text of the New Testament, the word for "generously" is *haplos*—meaning "bountifully" or "liberally." This means that when you pray, "God, please give me the wisdom I need to be the kind of woman and mother to positively influence and impact my daughter's life," God's response is not, "Well, all right, but only a little bit. Because

I'd rather save some wisdom for someone else who might really use it." No, that would be a stingy God. His response is also not, "I'll give you just a dose and if you use it wisely, then I'll give you more." The verse says He gives wisdom liberally—without reservation. He gives all we need, perhaps even *more* than we need, simply because we asked. God is not a cheapskate when it comes to giving us what He wants us to have.

2. He gives wisdom to us "without finding fault"

This means when we ask Him, in faith, for the wisdom and discernment that we need to be an encouraging mom, His reaction will not be, "Well, let's look at your track record of how wise you've been in the past. I mean, are you going to *use* the wisdom, or just rely on your same old ways and make the same old mistakes?" Nor is His response going to be, "You know, you always ask Me for something when you're in a pinch but then you end up doing your own thing, anyway." Nor will His response be, "But you are a lousy mom, so even My wisdom won't help you."

Nope. James 1:5 says God gives wisdom not only generously, but *without finding fault*. It's not critique time. It's not "Earn your right to it" or "Prove to Me you'll use it" or even "You've been foolish thus far, haven't you? I'm glad you're finally asking for help." He will give without listing your past faults. Now that's the kind of God I want to ask help from, don't you?

3. He gives wisdom to us when we ask for it, in faith

This shouldn't be a surprise. Back in chapter 1, we looked at how we can approach God boldly with our requests when we ask in faith and know that He hears us. James 1:6 clarifies the promise in James 1:5 (which is why we can't just take one verse and "claim it"—we have to look at what the whole passage is saying). James 1:6 tells us, "When you ask, you must believe and not doubt, because the one who doubts is like a wave of the sea, blown and tossed by the wind."

My friend, not only does God give *generously* and *without finding fault*, but when you ask Him in faith, He is your greatest cheerleader and coach whom you can trust for help. He is, after all, the one who appointed *you* to be your daughter's mom. Surely He is standing by to give you the wisdom and discernment you need to build her up into the woman He desires for her to become.

"Sometimes I'm Not Okay"

Lauren, now 23, was adopted as a baby into a loving family in ministry. But she realizes that, in spite of the loving and faithful parenting she received all her life, she still had a deeply ingrained need for acceptance and a sense of identity:

"In my high school years I struggled a lot with identity. Because I'm adopted, I searched a lot for who I was. During those times of searching I wish my mom could have seen through my facade of 'I'm okay' and realized I was struggling with who I was and wanting to feel accepted. I know she tried to help me and in a lot of ways she did, by showing me information about my adoption. But, in the end, I was scared to disappoint her by saying anything about my struggles. Now I realize that would not have been the case at all, but I was insecure then."

Yet in spite of those teen-year struggles, Lauren had a mom who was continuing to build her up through prayer and being available to answer the questions she had.

"My mom did a great job of building me up in a godly way, yet also letting me find my own faith. She was always good about giving me biblical history and background into things I had questions about. But most of all, she loved me unconditionally and was patient with me. I wouldn't trade her for anything. God knew the mother I was supposed to have, and He gave me the best. I'm so thankful for her. *So* thankful.

"I'm not yet a mom, but when I am, I hope to be as awesome of a mother as my mom was. Kind, gentle-hearted, compassionate, loving, and awesome. I try to be that woman with my husband."

Sara, Lauren's mom, encouraged Lauren's heart by taking time to answer her questions and by being a spiritual mentor to her. She says this of Lauren's upbringing: "I think Lauren might say that I was the kind of mom who talked with her a lot. I took time to explain life to her and sought to impart wisdom. I talked a lot about the difference Jesus makes in our lives and how much He loved her and wanted her to trust and obey

Him. Lauren was raised with lots of prayer with and for her. Turning to God in times of need by praying together about everything as a practice and habit was normal in our home."

There are so many things our daughters may need to hear from us. There are so many ways we can encourage them that we might not realize. With that in mind, let me share with you an eye-opening and heartbreaking account of what Kelly, now 30 years old, needed from her mother but never received. I include her story here because it serves as a warning and a gentle reminder to every mom of how very important it is to our daughters that we be their No. 1 cheerleader rather than their harshest critic. Sometimes, in our efforts to instruct our daughters or keep them from a prideful spirit, we simply withhold praise or only tell them how they can improve, or worse yet, say nothing. Listen to Kelly as she bares her heart.

······················· From Her Perspective ·······················

"I Wish I Could've Heard Her Say, 'Good Job'"

needed my mom to encourage and validate me—not fawn over me or give me a false sense of self. I know my mom said I was smart. She didn't say it a lot or even regularly, but I remember it. However, I can't remember my mom using any other positive words to describe me. She never said I was creative. She never said I was helpful or compassionate. She never called me pretty or graceful or athletic. I don't remember getting much positive feedback for anything. The honor roll, the writing awards, the marketing program success, being named manager of our school store, the acceptance in the honor program at college…it all seemed expected. And sometimes it never seemed good enough.

"I will never forget a conversation I had with my mom shortly before I got married. I was at my last dress fitting. I felt beautiful standing there with my wedding dress on. Then while I was putting my regular clothes back on, I mentioned that my 15-year-old second cousin was going to look so pretty in her bridesmaid dress. My mom replied, 'She will be the most beautiful girl at the wedding.' I replied, 'Besides me, right?' And my mom responded, with all seriousness, 'No. Alicia is much prettier than you. Why would you be prettier than her?'

"Now, I didn't really expect to be the best-looking woman anywhere. But it would have been nice for my mom to make me feel special, at least just this one time. But no—it was always someone else who was smarter, prettier, nicer, more creative, or better. I often asked myself, *Is there nothing I am good enough at?*

"My mom always went out of her way to show love and compassion to her mom, friends, sisters, neighbors, and even strangers. Yet I can't remember one time when she did that for me. I do remember my mom asking me to pick my favorite meal on my birthday and letting me have a nice dessert. My dad did the rest of the heavy lifting emotionally. He planned birthday parties, picked out special gifts, made forts in my bedroom when I was sick, and talked endlessly with me about the topics I loved. My mom was at my choir concerts, award banquets, and volleyball games. In fact, she missed only one event while I was growing up. However, I honestly couldn't tell you if she was proud of me or my achievements, or if she even wanted to be there.

"I would have loved to have known she thought I was a pretty neat person. I would have loved for her to say she thought I was good at something or was a good person or maybe that she was even proud of me.

"When I overcame my extremely shy nature at 14, I joined an organization of marketing students, entered a competition, and won something. Even a quick 'Good job' would have lifted me up in ways I can't even imagine. But I never heard it. And then, at the end of high school, when I continued with that organization and won lots of other awards, managed our school store, and spent day after day mentoring other students, it would have been nice to hear her say, 'Job well done.'

"When I was just a third grader and wrote an essay about my uncle's alcohol rehabilitation and received an award for it, it would have been awesome to hear from my mom that it was a great piece. Instead, I heard her tell others at the award ceremony about my uncle's accomplishments, which were deserved, but nothing about what I did. I was nine. I was so excited about my uncle that I wrote about him. But I ached to know my mom loved *me* too."

. . . .

Mom, don't let it ever be said that you didn't say the words your daughter needed to hear. Don't let it ever be read that you refused to give her what she needed most. Encourage her heart, build her up, let her know *she* is your greatest treasure and accomplishment. No matter how hard you try, you cannot spoil your daughter with love and praise. You can, however, without even realizing it, leave her aching for so much more.

Building Up Your Daughter

1. Which of the "whatevers" on page 63 do you most need to focus on so that you can build up your daughter with your words? Write out one practical way you will apply that "whatever" to your speech or conduct:

2. Make it a goal to apply Philippians 4:8 by saying only what is true, noble, right, pure, lovely, and admirable to your daughter—and others—for a whole day. You might find there are some things you can't talk about with her or others until you find a way to say them in accordance with this verse. That is a good lesson in taming the tongue. Once you master a day, try it for a week. You will be putting into practice a lifestyle that honors Christ in word and deed.

3. Consider purchasing a pretty journal. Put your daughter's picture on the cover (or just inside the cover) and let her know it is your prayer journal specifically for *her* prayer needs. Tell her it will be available for her at any time to write in it whatever she would like you to pray about. Tell her you won't bring it up in conversation with her, but only in conversation with God. This will make it a safe place for her to let you know what is going on and what she needs prayer about. It is a way for you to hear her heart.

You may also want to provide a section where she can indicate when the prayer was answered or the situation she asked you to pray about was resolved. This project will not only convince her of your praying heart for her, but it will help her see, firsthand, the power of prayer... and especially, the power of a *mother's* prayers. This is the type of project that helps a mom build a legacy of encouragement in her daughter's life.

My #1 prayer!

A Prayer to Encourage Her Heart

Lord, I commit to You my desire to build up my daughter in every way. Let no unwholesome word come out of my mouth, but only words that build her up, according to the need of the moment. Don't let me miss opportunities to praise or affirm her. And don't let me remain silent in those moments when she longs to hear words of affirmation, understanding, or love. Help me to build her up through my actions as well by coming alongside her and partnering with her in accomplishing her goals. May she remember me as the person in her life who encouraged her heart and built up her confidence in You and what she can accomplish through You.

Chapter 4

Giving Her the Gift of Your Time

Teach us to realize the brevity of life,
so that we may grow in wisdom.

PSALM 90:12 NLT

While going through Dana's backpack when she was in second grade, I found a paper on which she had written her spelling words for the week. I was pleased to see an "A" for correct spelling and grammar. (That's my girl!) But as I read her sentences, I discovered what I had become in her eyes:

> Busy—My mom is always so *busy*.
> Time—My mom never has enough *time*.
> Speed—My mom does things with such *speed*.
> Garden—My mom used to spend time in the *garden*.

My heart sank as I continued to stare at her paper. *Is this how she sees me?* I asked myself. Someone who is busy, never has enough time, speeds through life, and used to spend time in the garden?

Instantly, I realized two things. The first was that, to my seven-year-old daughter, I was her whole world. Every sentence was about her mom. She observed me. She studied me. I was the one she had written about. And the second was that she saw me as busy. That made me cringe. She saw me as a mom who was rushing through life, not as one who took the time to *be* with her.

How I longed, in that moment, for those sentences to read differently: My mom is never too *busy* for me.

My mom always makes *time* for me.

My mom runs to me with such *speed*.

My mom and I enjoy spending time in the *garden*.

Yet I realized if those sentences were to change, *I* would have to change.

I took a good hard look at my life that evening, after Dana went to bed. And I repented. I thought about what I want to teach my daughter and what I was inevitably showing her from my life. I prayed, "Lord, I don't want my daughter to see me as someone who rushes through life and has no time for her. Help me to realize I only have so much time left to influence her in a positive way and to show her that she is more important to me than anything else."

About eight months later, I sat with Dana's third grade teacher at a different school in the town where we had just moved. It was a routine, beginning-of-the-year parent-teacher conference. Dana's teacher, Mrs. May, happened to be a woman from my church whom I had taught in a discipleship group a few months earlier. She said to me, "Dana loves you so much. She tells me every day what you are doing and all that you're involved in. She is so proud of what you do."

I'm sure Mrs. May intended to give me a compliment by sharing with me that Dana talked often of what I did. But the words *doing* and *do* pierced my heart deeply. I wanted Dana to be proud of who I *am*, not necessarily what I *do*. I wanted her to talk of what we were doing *together*, not just about what her mother was doing, as she looked on from a distance. Again, it was right in front of my eyes that my rushing around, my busyness, my "doing" was what had made the biggest impression on her.

So again I found myself on my face before God: "Lord, I don't want to be a mom who is all about what I do, but not involved in my daughter's life. Don't let me rush through her childhood, focusing more on my life than hers. Help me to see that only a few things in life really matter, and she is one of them."

It was then that God opened up my eyes to Psalm 90:12, a verse that became a guiding factor in my life from that point on:

> Teach us to number our days,
> That we may gain a heart of wisdom.

Numbering Our Days

Dana's spelling sentences and the words spoken by her teacher were just two incidents—over the span of about a year—that showed me I needed to start "numbering my days" by slowing down, seizing the day, and focusing on the few things that mattered in life, my daughter being one of them. There were many more lessons God taught me during the next few years and I ended up including them in a book I wrote, titled *When Women Long for Rest*. Primarily, God began to show me He would rather have me spend time *with* Him than do a bunch of things *for* Him. And likewise, He was showing me that as a mom it was more important for me to be *with* Dana than do a bunch of things that were indirectly *for* her. God was impressing upon my heart that life was about relationship— with Him and with those whom I love. And I was missing it.

By the grace of God I was able to see, while Dana was still young, how I was rushing through life and missing so much of it with her. And I was able to make the necessary adjustments to slow down, seize the day, and play with her while she still wanted me around.

I know as I mention that, you may be experiencing heartache. Having not given our children the time they needed is a very real issue in the lives of many moms today, whether you're a busy mom with young children still at home, a working single mom who wants to spend far more time with your children than you can, or a mom whose children are grown and you're wishing you could turn back the clock. But just as I made certain changes in my life when Dana was eight, you can make them too, regardless of your daughter's age.

A Look at Our Regrets

If you need more convincing that time spent with your children is something you will never regret, look at some of the responses that moms gave me when I asked them "What do you feel you didn't do well as a mom?"

- "I don't feel I was as attentive with her as I wanted to be."
- "It was easy to get caught up in my work and not do the most important thing: simply be mom."

- "I don't feel I gave her enough of my time."
- "I didn't play enough with my daughter."
- "I felt like I put her in the care of others too much. I was not strong enough in my own person to always do right by them with regard to my job."
- "I feel I could've spent more quality time with her. I tend to get fussy about all the things I have to do, and I should've let the dishes pile up more when she was younger."

Those words, spoken in hindsight, implied that moms were wishing they had given their daughters more of themselves. More of their time, their interest, their support, their presence.

I don't believe a little girl—or a grown one—needs to have "quality time" as her love language in order to want her mother's time. Every little girl or young woman needs to know she is important to her mom.

Now that you've read the regrets from moms who wished they had spent more time with their daughters, let's take a moment to look at the responses from young women (ages 18–25) who have close relationships with their moms today.

What's Important to Her

Lauren, 22, says, "My mom made time for me and valued my opinion at a young age. Even though as a teenager I thought mother-daughter dates were lame, they are some of the best memories I have, and those times allowed us to really get to know each other."

Christen, age 23, has a close relationship with her mother today and shares how it developed: "My mom stayed home with her kids. She sacrificed a career to spend all day, every day, with me and my siblings. She gave all she had to us, and many times received nothing but heartache in return. She laid down her life daily, and continues to do so, in order to disciple her children in the ways of the Lord. I want to do that with my own children someday."

And Christen's mom, Susan, says this about her relationship with her daughter today: "My relationship with Christen is one of the best parts of my life. I look forward to spending time with her and I enjoy her company.

I find that we have much in common and we have fun together, not only as mother and daughter, but as friends. Our strengths are that we can talk easily and share openly. We share a common faith, which is the foundation of our relationship."

Susan says this relationship with her daughter developed because "I made dates for Christen and me to spend time together apart from my other kids. I was always open to having her friends at the house for just a day or for weekend-long sleepovers. I drove her to whatever activities and events in which she wanted to participate."

Susan had the advantage of being able to stay home full-time with her children and invest time in them daily. I realize not every mom has that luxury, especially if you're a single mom or if you have a husband who is unemployed, disabled, or in some way unable to work for the two of you. But our children are discerning. They know when a mom is gone out of necessity and when she is there but wishing she wasn't.

One grown daughter who is now a mother said this about her stay-at-home mom: "My mom always seemed so uptight. I remember always being told things to do or to just go play. She could have enjoyed her children more, but I know now that she didn't know how. She was an only child and had no idea how to invest her time in her children. We had no mother-daughter talks or anything close or personal."

What It Teaches Her

Regardless of your daughter's age, she desires the gift of your time. When she's little, she wants you to play with her. As she gets older, she wants you to shop with her. And as she moves out and has a life of her own, she still wants you to call and ask how it's going. She will always need the gift of your time. And it's never too early—or too late—to start giving it. When you give your time to your daughter, and not just your words, you are showing and teaching her three important truths:

- that she is a priority in your life
- how she can prioritize people in *her* life
- how she can enjoy life and not rush through it

Your Time Shows Her that She Is a Priority

As the director of women's ministries at my church for several years, I often had to tell Dana, and show her by example, that she really was "the most important little woman in mom's ministry to women." What good was I, as a leader of women in my church, if I took no time to direct, lead, guide, pray for, and spend time with the one young woman in my home? I remember, on at least one occasion, Dana had to remind me of my priorities when she was talking and my eyes were glued to my computer screen. As I recall, her words were, "Hey, mom, remember how you said I was the most important woman in your ministry to women?" Hearing my own words spoken back at me sure got me to turn around and focus on her!

Your Time Shows Her How to Prioritize Others

When you spend time with your daughter and teach her that people are more important than productivity, you are teaching her to spend time with her own children someday. Do you want your daughter to eventually be someone who is all about the task and to-do list? Or do you want her to be someone who takes time for others? She will most likely model what she sees in you. So show her someone who takes time for people by taking that time for her.

Your Time Teaches Her to Not Rush Through Life

When you give your daughter the gift of your time, you are showing her that life is about relationships and that people are more important than productivity. I had to ask myself, while Dana was growing up, if she would remember me as a woman always in a hurry, or a woman fixed on being holy. I want the latter to be true. And therefore, I had to carefully take notice of the number of times I said things like, "Hurry up," "Go faster," "We don't have time for this," and "We're going to be late." Instead, I wanted to be a mom who incorporated a little more "Slow down, honey, we have time," and "That's okay, we can wait." To this day, Dana still starts to tense up a little and look nervous when we are somewhere together and we are told how long a wait will be or we are asked to wait a little longer for something. I've noticed she relaxes quite a bit if she hears me cheerfully say, "No problem; we can wait."

My most enjoyable times with my daughter have been the days when I have pushed my workload aside and didn't watch the clock or my watch, and didn't worry about what I needed to do. Instead, I took the time to enjoy life with her. And this is something I want my daughter to learn—that life is not all about doing, it's about living. We were created to love God and enjoy Him forever. But if we don't know how to relax and enjoy life, or enjoy one another, how will we ever learn to enjoy God's presence? And how will our grown daughters ever learn to enjoy being with God or spending time with us, for that matter?

Chery says this, in hindsight, about her 21-year-old daughter, Chrystal, who tends to burn the midnight oil and not listen to her body's need for rest: "I wish I had taught my daughter to go to bed! Her work ethic is almost too good and I think that is a reflection of her watching me trying to keep up with things by overworking. I wonder now if I didn't teach her how to rest and trust God with what she couldn't get done in an evening."

Interestingly, when I asked Chrystal what her mom could have done better while raising her, she said, "It isn't something she could have done better for me, but for herself. She was constantly stressed by the tasks she faced every day. She was a stay-at-home mom while I was growing up, but I could tell she always had a lot on her plate. She always made time for me, but I wish I could have somehow helped to lessen the load for her."

Our daughters pick up on our stress. And they tend to imitate our approach to life. If we're hard workers, they will be too. That's not necessarily a negative. But they need to see us take time to just relax too, if they're going to incorporate rest in their own lives as well. Giving your daughter the gift of time doesn't just mean spending time with her. It means giving her an awareness of the need for rest and an example of how to enjoy life rather than work away every minute of it.

Making the Time

So how do you find the time to spend with your daughter? You can't. Time can't be *found* anywhere these days. We *make* the time for what is most important to us. As soon as your schedule frees up, something else will come up. Therefore, you and I must be deliberate and intentional about spending time with those we love the most. Here are some practical ways to start giving your daughter the gift of your time. It's really a matter of looking, listening, and learning.

1. Look for opportunities to do something special with her.

Although your daughter needs you on a daily basis, having specially planned weekly dates or monthly outings go a long way in letting her know she's important. Dana and I like to have something to look forward to that we can do together. It was that way when she was young, and it still is today. Sometimes I'll tell her on a Sunday afternoon, as she's leaving for the one-hour drive back to college, that I'll come that Wednesday or the following week for a lunch date and shopping. We both look forward to those times now.

Here are some ways you can do something special with or for your daughter to show her she's a priority in your life. If she is young and attends school:

- Sign up to help out regularly in her school classroom.
- Volunteer to drive for and/or chaperone her field trips.
- Stay *during* her after-school lesson or sports practice, watching her, rather than stopping by to pick her up later. (Even if you do this just once in a while, it will make an impact on her.)

If she is older and/or driving by now or living on her own:

- Buy tickets to a play, concert, or special attraction that the two of you can attend together.
- Schedule a weekly or monthly lunch with her (even if she's still living at home).
- Take her shopping for her or her children.
- Suggest a book or Bible study the two of you can do together (even if over the phone).
- Talk once a week via phone if she lives far away.

2. Listen for what's important to her and join her there.

Is your daughter talking about something a lot? That means it's important to her. Ask her questions about it, which will show your interest, but avoid the tendency to give your opinion or criticize quickly. We will look in the next chapter at a practical way to look at what's important to her and join her there.

3. Learn how to draw her heart closer to yours.

Become a student of your daughter. Study her. Learn what resonates with her heart and invest in it. Pick up on the little things she likes and start incorporating them into your day or week. Whatever takes time and is spent on her will translate to her that she is important to you.

When Dana was in elementary school, she got very excited when a popular chain of donut shops came to town. Now, I wasn't interested in donuts (well I *was*, but not in their calorie and fat count!). But a fourth-grader isn't counting calories (at least she shouldn't be overly concerned about them!). So we went to the new shop during its grand opening. She was absolutely thrilled as she watched how the donuts were made and picked out two for her and one for me. (I even splurged and paid $2 each for a glass of milk just so we could drink milk together with our donuts!)

Now, ordinarily I would've balked at paying that much for a glass of milk and the low nutritional value of the food. But a memory was made with Dana that day. We ended up going back during Dana's Christmas and summer breaks from school (that place gave a free donut for every "A" schoolchildren in town received on their report cards, which stocked us up on donuts for a while). And we would stop by if it were time for another "memory"—not because the donuts were healthy or a great value, but because Dana loved it.

Today, Dana steers clear of donuts (because of her interest in nutritional value and, more recently, a medical order to avoid wheat). But she still fondly remembers our dates at the donut place. For that, our visits were well worthwhile.

4. Lose the phone.

I have to say it: Put down the phone. I have regretted many times taking a call when my daughter was talking to me and realizing later, after seeing the look on her face, that she saw clearly she had been "bumped" by someone else I appeared to consider more important than her. If you are expecting an important call during the time you are spending with your daughter, tell her in advance, even ask her permission to take the call. Many times just acknowledging that her presence and feelings are important to you will smooth over any hurt feelings that your calls are more important than her presence. Ask "Do you mind if I take this call?" just like you would if you were having a conversation with a friend or coworker. That will help your daughter to see that she's not really being pushed aside for someone else. But an even better choice is to leave your phone at home, turn it off, or set it on silent.

Seizing the Day

One thing Dana will tell you today is that her mother knows how to seize the day. After years of working away what could have been memories and having little to show for that "busy work," I now realize that time is short. I have learned the wisdom behind Psalm 90:12: "Teach us to realize the brevity of life, so that we may grow in wisdom" (NLT).

These days, when Dana calls, I'm there. If she wants to talk, I'm in the moment. If there's work piling up for me to do and she's home for the weekend, the work can wait until I've spent time with her and she returns to school. If she's homesick and missing some time with me, I'll drive the 90-minute trip to have lunch with her and hang out for a while. Partly because I'm making up for what I didn't do so well when she was younger. Partly because I realize even her college years will fly by and I don't want to miss any more of them than I absolutely have to. And partly because I've finally realized life is short and I must seize the day to be with my daughter while she still wants me around.

Dana says, "Being an only child, it is somewhat easier for my mom to give me her complete attention than it would be for a mother of three or four children. Yet I love that when we are together, it seems as though nothing else matters. My mom will still stop what she's doing to go pick up lunch for me or drive 90 minutes to my college just to have lunch with me and shop."

When I read those words on the survey I asked Dana to fill out for this book, tears came to my eyes. They were tears of thankfulness to God for impressing upon my heart, 12 short years ago, that verse about numbering my days. Had God not opened my eyes up to how fleeting life is, my daughter could very well have said, "I wish my mom considered me important enough to drop whatever she is doing and spend a little time with me."

I am a firm believer that it is never too late to start seizing the day with your daughter. If you have more than one daughter, plan times of showing each one how very special she is to you. If your daughter is off at college, text her every now and then and let her know how much you think of her…and always will, no matter where she is and what she's doing. If she is half a world away, start writing her letters and expressing what you'd love to be doing if she were there with you in that moment.

And if you're a mom with a full plate or a full-time job and your heart is breaking right now as you're thinking, *I don't know where I'm going to find this time,* don't lose heart. Jean, a mother of five daughters ages 2–11, says this: "The ratio of daughters to mom is 5:1 and it can be challenging sometimes to set aside the amount of time I'd like to have with each child. So those one-on-one times are often spent during errands, meal preparation, and chore time."

Jean makes a point of noticing what each daughter is doing throughout the day or evening and commenting on it, asking her daughters what they enjoy, what they are thinking, and what is on their hearts.

Be creative. Find a way. Your schedule can wait. Your relationship with your daughter can't.

Before You Know It…

My friend Cheri Gregory posted this on her blog about six months before her daughter, Annemarie, left for college. I think it's a great reminder to all of us that our daughters won't be around forever. Before we know it, they'll be out the door, pursuing their schooling, dreams, or careers. And we must seize the day to give them our time while they are still around and asking for it. Listen to Cheri's heart, learn from it, and love your daughter while she's still within arm's—or ear's—reach:

"Already Missing"

Annemarie turned 18 last Wednesday.

My *baby* turned 18!

I've known this day would come. The goal of mothering is to work myself out of a job, and I've *calmly* anticipated the inevitable.

Until this year.

In January, on a stressful day, Annemarie asked if we could run to Jamba Juice. "I'm too busy!" I protested. Then it struck me: In September, she heads to college. Only eight more months till I start missing all the mother/daughter stuff we do. I dropped my busyness; we jetted to Jamba Juice.

Last week, I missed celebrating Annemarie's birthday because she's been on a mission trip in Belize since March 19. I thought I'd be fine while she was gone, as I was busy speaking for a women's retreat.

But throughout the weekend, I missed my constant companion. Annemarie always sets up my book table ("Stay away, Mum; you'll mess it up!"). She fusses over me ("You haven't eaten since breakfast! Go *eat*!"). And she's my biggest cheerleader ("You sure had them listening *and* laughing, Mum!").

And by Wednesday, I was *missing* my daughter something fierce. For all my bravado ("Your bedroom becomes my new craft room!"), I didn't realize how much I depend on calling out, "Hey Chickie?!" and hearing back "Yeah, Mum?" Or how much I rely on Annemarie being a text message away. She's been gone for just ten days, and ohhhh, how I miss my "baby"!

Annemarie returns home Monday evening, and I can't wait to welcome her back. As soon as she's caught up on sleep, we'll head to Jamba Juice so she can tell me about everything I missed.

And then I'll blink: It'll be May 31, and I'll get misty-eyed at "Pomp and Circumstance." Then I'll blink again: It'll be mid-September, and I'll be overstaying my welcome in her dorm room.

I wouldn't have missed the last 18 years for anything in the world. And for the next few months, I'm going to do my best not to miss a thing.

Annemarie may not leave till September, but one thing I've learned is that a part of me—of my heart—goes with her.

And that part of my heart is already missing.[10]

••••••••••••••••

I wanted to close this chapter by letting you hear from Cheri's daughter Annemarie, who is now 21, living away from home, and missing her mom.

•••••••••••••••••• From Her Perspective ••••••••••••••••••

"She Gave Me Her Time by Listening"

My mom met my expectations of a mom by constantly listening to me. That's half the battle, I think. She would listen, and often while I was talking or thinking things through I would come to a conclusion I wouldn't have otherwise. Her taking so much time to listen to me meant that she really did care, even if she didn't understand. She failed to meet these expectations when she didn't respond to me—listening is great, but when she would simply nod or 'Mm-hmm' along, I would falter and stop talking or stop trying to make sense of it. There's not really a wrong thing to say—I mean, there is, but talking is better than not at all, from my perspective. I needed her to be involved, and when she would talk back to me (sometimes she would play devil's advocate in order to help me understand a problem, or she would repeat back to me what she heard to make sure she understood what I was saying), it was always helpful.

"What meant the most to me wasn't hearing that she was proud of me, though that was great, and it wasn't knowing that she supported me, though that was great too. It was her sitting and listening and trying to help me make sense of whatever had happened or whatever was going on. Knowing she was with me to figure and fight things out made all the difference in the world.

"I value our frequent communication. In a world where both of us are very, very busy—and are easily overwhelmed by the demands of our day-to-day work, not to mention family and friends—I value the fact that we continually make an effort to keep in contact with each other. It doesn't have to be much—sometimes it's only a text about some silly thing the cat did at home, and other times it's a detailed response to a lengthy email I wrote. But it goes back to knowing she's in my corner. Whenever we talk (or send silly pictures or small texts or advice on a situation), it's an affirmation that she is with me, and making an effort to be.

"What did my mom do best? She listened. She listened to *me*. I cannot count the number of times I was whining about schoolwork or crying about a boy or wondering whether or not the girls in my class liked me or where I was going to go after graduation or asking for another nail polish color. It feels like a lot of what I have talked to my mom about in my life isn't what matters. But she stayed, and she listened, and she still listens. So few people do that anymore today. And I know it's in the job description of a mom. But she has her own life, her own plans, her own hopes, and her own work—and she'll still sit down to listen to me talk about my best friend who I miss because he's in Africa, or she'll Skype with me about how my week went, or she'll nonchalantly mention that of course she and dad will drive me to Chicago when I go to graduate school there, or she'll write an email in response to some confusing thoughts I had, or she'll listen to me talk about my art thesis while we're driving.

"My mom listens. And again, even if she doesn't always agree with or doesn't understand me, at least she listens and she tries. Showing me that respect has made me respect *her* more."

•••••••••••••••

Now is the time. You will never regret the actions you take to reprioritize your life and start giving your daughter the gift of your time. As you do, chances are that when she is older, she'll generously give you the gift of *her* time too.

Spending Time with Your Daughter ··································

1. Ask your daughter what three words would best describe you. If *busy* is one of them, that may be an indication of what is impacting her the most right now. Ask her what you can do to let her know you are never too busy for her. Sometimes just opening the dialogue can lead to healthy discussions and reveal the hidden hopes of her heart.

2. Read and reflect on the following verses. Then write a brief response to each one in terms of your relationship with your daughter:

   Psalm 90:12—

   Matthew 6:19-21—

   Matthew 22:37-39—

3. Take the time right now…that's right, put the book down and right now…go check on her and see what she's doing (whether that means walking into her room and getting on the floor and playing with her, or planning an activity with her or picking up the phone and texting or calling her to say she is on your mind).

A Prayer for Prioritizing Your Daughter

Lord, You have never pushed me aside for "more important things" to do, or even told me, "Wait until I have time." May I model to my daughter the way You have deliberately and intentionally loved me. Give me the wisdom to number my days so I can live wisely, making each moment with her count and storing up memories in her mind and treasures in her heart. May she be convinced that nothing is more important to me than spending time with her. If You must, rearrange my life so that I will make the changes now that need to be made. And help me to live each day with the realization that I have only so much time left to love her, support her, listen to her, and cheer her on.

Chapter 5

Taking an Interest in Her World

The purposes of a person's heart are deep waters,
but one who has insight draws them out.

PROVERBS 20:5

C hristi Kari had a remarkable relationship with her mom.
Although she was raised during the 1960s and '70s—an era in which stay-at-home moms were being told that there's more to life than just being a wife and mother—Christi never felt she was a bother, burden, or hindrance to her mother. To the contrary, she felt loved, accepted, and supported by her mom because of the way her mom took an interest in her world.

"Both of my parents spent large amounts of time with my friends and my two brothers' friends," Christi said. "They took all of us to the lake, had numerous parties at our house, and took all of us on camping trips. Those friends love my parents to this day."

But what Christi loved the most was that her mom was intimately acquainted with her world.

"My mom got me involved in lots of activities—4-H, flute lessons, pageants, cheerleading, and so on, which gave me opportunities to meet people and experience new things, and grow in maturity and confidence. And by doing so, she spent valuable time with me.

"We were like best friends, even during my teen years. I honestly feel that all the good that lies within me is a direct result of her making me feel like I could do anything I set my mind to do," says Christi, who is a wife, mother of two adopted children, and an author of several books.

Today, Christi seeks to imitate her mother's example as she cares for her own daughter, now 15. Here's what she does:

- "I ask about her school day when I pick her up."
- "I make sure I know who her friends are, and even what their parents are like."
- "I take her to school activities."
- "I take her and her boyfriend and friends to many activities."
- "I watch the movies she watches and listen to the music she listens to just so I have an idea of what's going on in her world."

Entering Her World

Spending time with our daughters is important, but not if it's only time doing what *we* want to do. To enter her world means leaving yours, temporarily, and entering the unfamiliar, awkward, and sometimes even threatening world of her generation, her interests, and her preferences.

Kay recalls that she spent many years involved in an activity that her mom never showed an interest in: "My mom would spend time with me in the areas that she liked or felt comfortable with instead of trying to sometimes understand how God wired me," Kay said. "For example, I played softball in town for ten summers with my friends from junior high through college. I am not sure that she ever came and watched a complete game. I have forgiven her and don't hold it against her. But I don't think either of us realized how important it was to me that she participate in my life in that way."

On the other hand, Chrystal had the full support of her mom when she became interested in horses: "My mother was supportive of my horse-back riding while I was growing up. She was there for every lesson and every visit to my horse. I really appreciated her taking the time to learn about what I loved and watch me grow in the sport."

Crossing over from your world of work, bills, finances, friends, responsibilities, and personal hobbies into what your daughter is interested in is a way that you can share her heart, reinforce to her that her interests are important to you, and become a more central figure in her life. (Maybe even become her most loyal supporter too.)

When She Seems Worlds Away

Sometimes, just because our daughters live in a different generation, we tend to stay out of their world and out of their way. These are some of the most common complaints I hear moms say in the course of any given day:

"I can't stand the music my daughter listens to."

"I don't understand why that look appeals to her."

"She wants me to be on Facebook, but I think it's silly and a waste of time."

"I don't know why it's so important for her to be doing this right now."

"I never liked anything like that when I was her age; I don't know why she does."

"She won't pick up the phone and talk with me. She prefers to text. And I can't, so we basically don't talk much."

Do you hear love in those statements, and a willingness to find a way? Or do you hear indifference or even a stubborn resistance? If you and I don't understand something our daughters are interested in, or don't prefer it for ourselves, we can sound critical of them without intending to. But our daughters are not us. They have different tastes than we do. They will enjoy things that we will not. And they will roll their eyes at things we think are cool. One of the best ways to convince your daughter that you are not out of touch with her world is to ask her questions about it, to be open-minded when it comes to things that are unfamiliar or seem strange to you, and to make an honest effort to be interested in her interests simply because you're interested in *her*.

When you first became interested in your husband, you would hang out in places you normally wouldn't simply because he was there, right? You would listen to him talk about things you weren't necessarily interested in because you were interested in *him*. The same principle applies with your daughter. Be in the places where she is and get to know what she's interested in if you truly want to share her world and show her that you care.

Tina was raised by a mom who never looked outside her own small world of self-fulfillment to take an interest in Tina's life. She tended to act selfish and was verbally abusive to Tina.

So Tina has made a priority of getting involved in her daughter's world by asking questions and taking an interest in what she doesn't understand.

"I found out that my daughter, Marie, is a great artist and loves anime. I'm clueless about anime, and she likes to explain it to me and sometimes we watch it together." Tina says that by paying attention to her daughter and asking her questions, she was able to discover something she wouldn't have known about Marie. She's now able to share something with her daughter that might have otherwise left her as the clueless mom on the sidelines. Tina's open mind and heart to something that she didn't readily understand formed a bridge into Marie's world. And now there is another place in her teenage daughter's world where she is not only invited, but is beginning to feel at home.

Find a Way

If your daughter is not living with you, or you work full-time, or it's been difficult to make time to be with her, find a way.

I discovered an interesting dynamic as I was interviewing mothers and daughters for this book. Some of the mother-daughter pairs who shared the closest relationships with each other were actually stepmom and stepdaughter. After investigating further, I noticed that those stepmoms had made a deliberate effort to get to know the daughters of their husbands. They put forth perhaps more of an effort than natural moms tend to because they were at a disadvantage of not being the *real* mom or the mom who was living with her.

As I think back on my own experience with my stepmom, Sharon, I can see this principle at work. Although she didn't become my stepmom until after I was married, and therefore I didn't have the experience of living with her, she has nonetheless grown close to me through her intentional efforts to take an interest in my world and be supportive of me at every turn. Whether you are your daughter's birth mom, adopted mom, foster mom, stepmom, or even grandmother, we all can learn from the "extra mile" that a couple of these stepmoms traveled to establish a close, trustworthy bond with their daughters that remains today.

As a stepmom, my friend Chris insisted that she and her husband be actively involved in his children's lives, even though it meant having to drive several hours and deal with sometimes uncomfortable situations with his ex-wife.

"While the kids were young and living with their mom, we subscribed to their local paper. We would watch for special events taking place in their town, and we would go out of our way to get there and take them and be a part of their lives with them," Chris said. "Anything they would do, we would be there."

At 13 years old, Cristina and her younger brother moved in with her dad and stepmom and continued to live with them until they moved out for college. And Chris continued to make the effort to be a part of her step-children's lives in any way she could.

"Whatever Cristina was into, I tried to show interest in it too," Chris said. "Because I was interested in *her*, I became interested in what she was interested in. And it wasn't just 'Here's the check, go sign up.' It was more like 'What do you need? Do you need me to go for you? Should we make some phone calls? How can I help with this?'"

Cristina adds, "She never stifled anything. If I was interested in vintage clothes, she would take me to vintage stores to try on vintage clothes." After a while, Cristina was convinced her stepmom really was interested in her life and was willing to do what it took to be a part of it.

Sherry experienced the same with her stepmom, Judy. Judy married Sherry's dad when Sherry was five years old, and about a year later, Sherry started spending every other weekend with them. Judy was careful not to try to "replace mom" because Sherry already had one. But having never had a daughter of her own (Judy has two sons), she wanted to make her relationship with Sherry a special one.

"The early years, while Sherry was growing up, we had a lot of fun together," Judy said. "I had always wanted a daughter, and we did lots of fun things together, like arts and crafts.

"When she was younger she was a little distant emotionally because we didn't get to see her that often. Our relationship was more on the surface. Today, we're closer emotionally because she's an adult. We can talk more about real-life situations, deeper things. We can go below the surface now. Yet we still have a lot of fun together."

Sherry agrees: "Today it's still a fun relationship. I look up to her as my mother. Our relationship is respectful and loving, yet I'm not afraid to goof off and be silly with her."

Sherry says she realizes now that Judy had "built a friendship with me before a mother-daughter relationship. She was loving and patient with me. She earned my trust before she ever tried to be a mother.

"I still love my mom a lot," Sherry said. But she has a special bond with her stepmom that she was never able to establish with her birth mom. And that is because Judy took it upon herself to enter Sherry's world and make it happen.

Getting Closer to Her Heart

By taking an interest in your daughter's world, you are not only finding ways to be with her, but you are also showing her that you are not on the sidelines, out of touch, and in the dark about her or her generation. You are, instead, a credible counselor and a source of valuable wisdom when she needs it.

One young woman who was raised by loving parents with high morals said this about her mom not understanding or entering her world: "I didn't feel like my mom understood my generation and could relate to me, so I was left without a mature mentor, which left me to fall under the influence of most of my peers, who like me, were experimenting in life—both good and bad."

Precious Mom, don't give your daughter the excuse or the belief that you don't understand or have a clue about her world. Instead, show her you are on top of it by either directly entering into her world or considering one of these detours.

Be the Driver

The mom of my daughter's sixth-grade friend, Erin, would often say, "I'm the driver" when it came to discussions about what our children were interested and involved in. At first I thought she was referring to a personality trait of hers or a method of controlling the circumstances. But she was being literal.

"No, I'm the *driver*," Cheri reiterated. "I will drive my daughter wherever she and her friends are planning to go. When I'm the driver, I'm the one who knows exactly what and where something is happening, who is there, and what everyone is dressed like. I get a chance to meet the other kids who are involved. And most importantly, I get to talk to her and her friends on the way to and from wherever it is they're going. Sometimes I just drive and listen and find out a lot. I get a clear insight into what they talk about, laugh about, or worry about. I get to see into their world a lot better when I'm the driver."

Once Cheri explained this to me, I had to start negotiating with Cheri to let *me* do some of the driving when both our girls wanted to go somewhere together. It was on those occasions that it ended up being us *four* who were in the car together!

When I was the driver on Dana's seventh-grade field trip, I got a sense for the peer pressure she was experiencing every day just by the conversation going on between her and her friends about what radio station to listen to in the car. Dana's "Christian radio" preference was a bit passé for the eighth graders in the car. I also learned, at that time, that Dana found it easier to back down to the others' requests rather than take a stand on her own.

That experience helped me and my husband in our decision of where to place Dana when she graduated from her small Christian middle school and entered high school. Her father and I didn't believe she was enough of a leader to put her in the midst of the huge public school in town, which had about 4000 students. We opted, instead, to enroll her in a Christian high school of about 400 students—which was already four times the size of the middle school she had just graduated from. During those four years at the Christian high school, Dana developed into one of the school's top leaders, and by the time she graduated, she had received several leadership scholarships for college. But most importantly, pressure to back down on her convictions and go with someone else's preferences today isn't even a second thought for her.

As her mom, it was my job to gauge where she was in terms of being a leader or a follower and in what situations she might flourish or flounder. And I was able to collect much of that information by being the driver.

I continued to be the driver when Dana joined the cheerleading squad in high school. Not only did I get to know all her friends that way, but I also sensed Dana's pleasure at having me present at each competition. Looking back now, those Saturday cheer competitions went so quickly her first two years of high school that I'm glad I never missed one. And because she ended up getting injured, and therefore sidelined from cheer competition during her junior and senior years, I'm glad I didn't put off till the next year any chance to get involved and be present in her world.

Be the Greeter

What if your daughter is older and doesn't need you to drive her anywhere? That's when you transition into the *greeter* stage—you become the one who meets her at the door at the end of the day to ask how it went or stays up late when she comes home in the evening. Many moms have told me that it's during the late night hours that their daughters or sons want to talk. My daughter was never one to bare her heart in the morning or even early in the day. In fact, it was often difficult to pull words out of her when I sensed she was bothered by something. But on occasion, when she'd arrive home at ten or eleven at night, I found that if I met her at the door in my robe or in the door of her bedroom or bathroom as she was getting ready for bed, she would want to talk. She was either too wired to sleep and was excited to share her day with me, or she was troubled and looking for someone to listen.

If you are no longer needed as the driver, then by all means, be the greeter.

Be the Caller

And if your daughter is now an adult and living on her own, be the caller. Be the one who initiates conversation as a way of saying, "I am still interested in your life more than you may realize." If your daughter is not one who answers her phone (yes, there are lots of daughters today who would rather text than talk!), then communicate in *her* preferred way. Text her a message to ask how she's doing, if she needs anything, or how you can be more supportive of whatever she's involved in. If she'd rather communicate through social media, or that's the only way she engages in conversation, learn it and be there. Find a way. Be a part of her world so your voice can be heard just as often and just as clearly as everyone else who is now in her world.

Entering and being a part of your daughter's world takes time. And it requires sacrifice. It may mean dropping what you have to do so you can be the driver. It might amount to getting a little less sleep so you can be the greeter. And it may require you to push your work aside and pick up the phone so you can be the caller. There might even be times when it means shelving your own interests and goals to give her a chance to pursue what is important to her. But when you realize it is only for a season, and that season will fly by so quickly, you'll want to do what you can to make her a priority in your life.

Share a Project Together

Nicole, a single mom, remembers her mother taking an interest in her world, and she realizes it is important for her to do the same with her daughter: "Mom and I bonded and spent a lot of time together making crafts and jewelry. We even sold our creations at local street fairs. Last year, I helped Mom sell her felt purses and bracelets at a craft fair, and then I got to blog about it. With my own daughter, I'd like to set aside more time for our 'crafternoons' as we call them. We go to a craft store and purchase inexpensive supplies with our coupons, and then go home to connect through creativity. I'm thrilled to pass on this tradition. It's also another experience to blog about!"

Look for Ways She Can Feel Included

Looking for a way your daughter can feel included or accepted is another way of taking an interest in her world.

I remember feeling like "the odd one out" because my mother and sister both excelled musically, but I didn't. I admit I even wondered at times if my mom was as proud of me as she was of my older sister, Kristi, who could play any instrument by ear (starting at the age of five!), just like my mom. Kristi had an exceptional voice and could sing in registers higher than I thought possible, just like my mom. I was an alto, however, who was often off key during childhood. And to this day, I still can't harmonize. Kristi could also draw well, like my mom. I could only draw stick figures.

Kristi was, in many ways, my mother's daughter. And I was my father's. But my mom was aware of the ways in which I was different and, as I look back now, I realize she helped me find my niche and be okay with the fact that I wasn't just like my sister, or just like her.

Though I couldn't play an instrument, I still wanted to be in the marching band like Kristi (who played any instrument that was needed at the moment!). So Mom suggested I take up baton twirling and began investing in what I needed for that by paying for my lessons and driving me all over to get my outfits and needed accessories.

She started me in baton lessons when I was in sixth grade, which is rather late for most baton twirlers. But by the beginning of seventh grade, I was the solo twirler in the junior high school marching band and I became the featured solo twirler all four years of high school, performing in the football game halftime shows and in parades and marching band competitions. It was the most fun I had in high school, and it happened because Mom realized I needed to feel accepted and included by finding an area in which I could excel. Mom continued to be supportive by letting me get a new glittery uniform every year and even investing in light and fire batons for me! (She drew the line at twirling knives, however!)

Do you sense a deep need in your daughter to feel accepted, to excel at something, or to just feel included in something everyone else seems to be able to do? Get creative. Think outside the box. Find a way to encourage her and help her stand out. It's one small way you can affirm her identity and her dreams.

Who Is It For?

While it is important to be involved in our daughter's world, we need to make sure we do so for our daughter's benefit…not our own. Too many moms push their daughters for their own agenda. To make sure we aren't guilty of that, we need to listen to our daughters along the way and be ready to help, not hinder them. And yes, I say this from personal experience.

When Dana was in middle school, she joined the cheerleading squad. *Oh, a cheerleader, how fun,* I remember thinking. I decided that, for her school picture that year, I would take her to a department store in her cheerleading uniform with megaphone and pom poms and get some cute poses there, instead of the typical pose in the school uniform, with boring grey background, which tended to look the same year after year. But shortly before it was time for her school picture appointment, Dana complained to me that she hated her life.

"You what?" I asked. How could a 12-year-old hate her life?

"I'm stressed out. I have way too much to do," she complained. Dana was involved in several activities that met weekly—a Bible club that involved memorization and extra projects; piano lessons; a singing, dance, and drama ministry; an interpretive dance ministry; and in addition to those weekly obligations plus school homework, she had daily cheer practice after school.

I asked her "What needs to go?" She immediately chose to drop cheer. "It's *every* day, Mom. I don't even have a chance to *live.*" (Yes, Dana tended to talk very dramatic like that, something she probably picked up from her mom.) So we let her drop cheer. And a few months later, we let her piano lessons go as well.

At first I was heartbroken—no cute cheer pictures this year. Then I had to ask myself: "Is this for *her,* or for me?" While I was also disappointed about letting Dana end her piano lessons (her grandmother had even been paying for them!), I realize, in retrospect, that letting those activities go was the best thing we could do for her at the time. Not only did she return to cheer in high school and excel at it by then, but after a cheer injury, she returned to her love for piano, remembering the fundamentals she had learned during her two years of lessons. Today, Dana is a beautifully accomplished musician on the piano *and* guitar. It was all in God's timing that she flourished in her interests and talents. Pushing them on her at a young age might have discouraged any further interest at all in cheer and playing music.

Help Her Focus

Besides eliminating stress in her life, reducing Dana's load also helped her focus on a few things and do them well. Too often we want to help our children find balance. But helping them balance themselves on a tightrope between a multitude of activities on either side of them, and hoping they don't fall, isn't helping them at all. It is teaching them, while young, to run at a pace that they can't possibly maintain when they're older. We need to teach our children that to be involved and committed to certain things also means being able to say no to other things.

To focus on one or two things and excel at them is better than to try to do (and excel at) everything. In fact, the more things your daughter does—and excels at—the more difficult it might be for her later to focus on the one or two things she does really well. (That might help explain why some college freshmen aren't sure what they want to major in. Having been exposed to *so many* things, they may need two to three years of college before they can focus and narrow down their interests and options.)

Instead of pushing or allowing our daughters to be involved in every activity that comes their way, we need to, instead, help them focus on the few things they do best. That will help them find focus later in life and more quickly understand the ways in which they excel.

Help Her Rest

If I want my daughter to succeed in her interests and pursuits, then she must know how to walk away from something that is demanding too much from her or adversely affecting her emotional, physical, or spiritual health. I must be the one who teaches her how to rest, and how to say no to other things that press in. I must teach her the principle that sometimes, less is better than more.

When Dana gave up cheer and piano, she was able to enjoy a little of her after-school time and simply be a child. The rest also helped her invest more energy into pursuing some awards in her Bible program and excelling in her onstage opportunities. It was also important to Dana that her mom not consider her a failure or a disappointment or a quitter for giving up a few pursuits that were stressing her out. To the contrary, I was proud of her for recognizing her limitations and choosing to do a few things well, rather than many things with mediocrity.

Continue the Interest

Sometimes we assume that our daughters only need us to be involved in their world when they are children—while they're young, they need our money, our driving skills, our affirmation and encouragement. But even after they've grown older and moved out, and they can support themselves and they have their own life, they still need us to care about and be interested in what they are doing. In fact, they need it far more than we may realize.

How can you and I continue to show interest in our daughters' lives? By keeping up with what they're interested in. Susan—whose 23-year-old daughter, Christen, is an early intervention specialist—says she stays connected with her daughter and continues to show an interest in her world by supporting Christen in her job and doing research for the children she serves.

"I also rise when she does (and sometimes even earlier) in order to make her breakfast, tea, and pack a lunch for her. I buy her toys for her job because they are expensive and she needs them. I enjoy being part of her life like that. I also make dates to be with her, such as for little vacation times, for getting our nails done, for meeting for coffee, and for doing a Bible study."

Pamela says this about staying connected with her 14-year-old daughter, Katie: "I try to daily engage my daughter in conversation. I try to take an interest in what she is doing, how she is feeling, or in what she likes or dislikes. I attempt to pay attention to details as she shares them. I ask questions to spur dialogue and to help me understand who she is and how she feels about her world, herself, and others."

Here are some things you and I can do to make sure our children never feel as though we've checked out of their world:

- No matter what her age, ask her, daily, how she is doing.

- Ask her at least weekly what you can do to help her in some way.

- Ask her often how you can pray for her. And then follow up by asking how she is doing in that area in which she requested prayer.

- Regardless of her age, ask what she's enjoying at this point in her life. Ask what she doesn't like. Ask what she struggles with. Offer advice, if asked. Otherwise, just listen.

Take an interest in her passions and pursuits no matter how old she is. She will never stop wanting you to be interested in and proud of her. And you will never regret the steps you took to bridge your different worlds.

"I Wish I Had More of Her Listening Ear"

One young woman, now 21, told me that her mom took a deep interest in her life starting when she was young. In fact, her mom sacrificed for her in many ways. But today, this young woman still needs her mom to be a listener and care about what she's doing now that she's living away from home and attending college.

"There's one thing I don't have anymore that I wish I still had (and I've told my mom this and she says she can't really do anything about it, which I now have peace about). When I call her, it's not about me, ironically. It's all about her. Though I need to have that communication, it is now focused on what is going on with her.

"I wish I had more of her listening ear. I've told her that for years, and we've talked about it at length. But she becomes defensive about it. I have come to realize I can only control myself and my emotions, and I've had to lower my expectations in that area. Now when I call her, I am expecting to just reconnect with her to find out what is going on in *her* life. But when I call my *dad*, the conversation will be about what I'm doing.

"I will email my mom about what's going on with me. I will tell her in the email how I'm doing. I feel dutiful to let her know what's going on in my life. I know she *wants* to know, but I know she won't think to *ask*."

·················

My heart goes out to that young lady who wishes she had her mother's listening ear. And, I realize that could so easily be *my* daughter saying those things if I am not consciously aware of the need to keep asking about her world and listening to and learning about her. I constantly need to remind myself, *Come out of your world and enter hers so the two of you won't drift apart.*

That young woman has maturely realized that her mom may always be that way. So she is going with the positive aspects of the relationship and not expecting from her mom what her mom can't give.

But *you* can be the mom whose daughter will be able to say, "My mom is genuinely interested in my world. She takes the time to understand me and learn what makes me tick so she can remain a relevant part of my life."

Investigating Her World

1. At this point in your daughter's life, which are you? (Circle one or more.)

   The Driver   The Greeter   The Caller

2. Which of the steps on page 101 are you willing to start doing today, and how?

3. List the tangible ways you are involved in your daughter's world right now.

A Prayer for Engaging in Her World

Lord, thank You for the diverse interests in my daughter's life. Please help me spend the time needed to discover what makes her heart beat, and help me to recognize ways in which I can share that part of her life with her. Help me to come out of my own world long enough to be a relevant part of hers and offer my love, support, and enthusiasm for the things she is interested in. Don't let my own preferences keep me from discovering more of what thrills her heart.

Chapter 6

Encouraging Her to Dream

God can do anything, you know—far more than you could
ever imagine or guess or request in your wildest dreams!

EPHESIANS 3:20 MSG

The first time my daughter heard me speak to women about discovering their dream, she acted like she wasn't listening. I assumed my 13-year-old had other things on her mind than having to listen to her mother's final retreat session before she could return home.

But on the heels of my presentation, Dana approached me, wide-eyed and full of anticipation, and said, "Now that you've told all these women how they can discover their dream, are you going to help me reach mine?"

"Of course, Dana," I responded. "What *is* your dream?"

My daughter had often talked of becoming an artist or professional dancer, and at times of being a veterinarian because of her love for animals. But her answer that day took me by surprise.

"I want to be an actress on the Disney Channel."

I said the first thing that often comes to a parent's sometimes-too-practical mind.

"Honey, *every* child your age wants to be on the Disney Channel. Do you know the chances of that happening?"

I saw her smile disappear and her eyes tear up, and I knew, instantly, the damage I'd caused in that one critical statement. After writing a book—and speaking for the past hour—on wounds that can destroy our dreams, I was becoming the Dream Destroyer right in front of my daughter's hopeful eyes.

"Oh, Dana, I'm sorry," I said, hoping to redeem the moment. "How could I even say such a thing after telling these women to dream big and trust their big God to come through for them?

"Let's start over," I continued. "You want to be an actress. Okay...let's talk about this. All your life you've loved the stage and people have loved *you* on the stage. You have a natural ability to sing, act, and dance. Your passion *is* acting. I've seen that in your school plays. So let's take this to God in prayer. Let's ask Him what *His* dream is for you."

Dana and I prayed that afternoon and that evening and the next that God would open the doors wide if acting was the dream He had for her. Or if it was the first step in whatever else He had for her. We prayed that Dana's intention would be not for her fame and glory, but for God's. We prayed that if Dana could be a light in this world by letting Jesus shine through her on stage, that He would reveal to us the next step. And we asked that God would "fling open a door" that we couldn't possibly miss so we'd know for sure it was from Him.

And fling open the doors He did.

That next weekend, while I was speaking, Dana happened to tell a woman named Jane that she wanted to be an actress someday. That woman enthusiastically responded by saying she had the same dream at Dana's age and prayed that God would do the impossible for her, and then recounted step by step all He did that landed Jane in a number of teen movie and television credits. Dana asked me if we could have lunch with Jane after the event that afternoon and talk some more, so we did. Jane was a fountain of boundless energy and encouragement and continued to direct Dana toward trusting her God. We thanked God—all the way home—for the encouragement He heaped on Dana's dreamer heart through Jane's words that day.

The next day, the second door flew open. And a couple days later, the third.

Less than a month later, Dana was one of 12 teenagers in the Southern California area accepted from a screen audition into an elite acting school. Within three months of entering the school, she had two callbacks, one from a talent agency and another from a business interested in her work. She continued to hone her skills, take acting lessons, and trust

God's timing as she gained what she needed to move to the next level of God's dream for her.

Today, Dana is not involved in television acting. But her training at the acting school was a first step in gaining the confidence, stage experience, and trust in God necessary to do what she believes is *God's* dream for her today: leading worship and public relations work with an emphasis on event planning. Her dream took shape over the course of about five years. And, incidentally, just before she started college, she considered attending a four-year performing arts academy in downtown Hollywood. While I had my reservations (and, I'll admit it, *fears*) about that choice but was careful not to express them, Dana told her father and me one evening that she didn't believe God wanted her in that acting academy after all. She believed He was calling her to focus more on music through an education at a private Christian university. Relieved, we supported her in that next step.

While Dana started college as a vocal performance music major, during her sophomore year she changed her major to public relations—a new major being offered that year—because of her strength in writing, public speaking, and event planning. Today she is a straight-A student, excelling in her new major, a leader on campus, the public relations director of the school's women's choir, and working her way through college as the Sunday morning worship leader at our church.

What Is *Your* Daughter's Dream?

Some daughters are dreamers. They come out of the womb, it seems, with big plans for what they want to accomplish with their lives. Dana is one of them. All her life she has talked of what she has wanted to do. And she aims high. But every daughter approaches life differently, and every daughter's dream is unique. That's why it's so important for you to pay close attention as a mom.

For some children, it's obvious what their calling is. For most, however, it can be a mystery—a secret worth pulling out of them.

One mom told me, "My high-school-aged daughters don't have dreams. They aren't motivated beyond the here and now and shopping and having a boyfriend. They're not really passionate about *anything*."

Some people are dreamers—it's part of their personality. They also tend to be entrepreneurial in spirit, high achievers, and goal oriented. Other people are more laid back. They are not big-picture in their thinking. They are not self-starters. But it doesn't mean they don't have dreams. Perhaps they just lack the confidence to dream big or verbally express their dreams. While some children know from the time they are young exactly what they want to do with their lives (I was one of them), others take a while to develop their creative abilities or academic interests. But by watching, and praying for wisdom to help cultivate that dream God has placed on their hearts, we can be there to be the wind beneath their wings when it's time for them to fly.

Seeing Her as God's Masterpiece

So what is all this talk about *God's* dream for your daughter? I think it starts with the dream He whispers on our hearts as little girls and from there it develops into what we would like to do with our lives. But we often don't know the two are related. We tend to think we have our own dreams for our lives and God eventually comes along and cooperates with them. But, to the contrary, I believe God places His wish on our hearts first.

For the past several years, I've been speaking on how a woman can discover her dream. And afterward, I often have women tell me that they never had a dream for their lives. When I ask if they were the oldest child in their family (or the oldest girl), 90 percent of the time that is the case. Then they admit that they were always taking care of everyone else and that they never really thought about what God wanted specifically for them.

Remembering She Is God's Masterpiece

It isn't selfish for you or me, or our daughters, to have dreams. It is natural. And I believe it is God-given. The Bible tells us, in Ephesians 2:10, "We are His workmanship, created in Christ Jesus for good works, which God prepared beforehand that we should walk in them" (NKJV).

The original Greek word that the King James Version and the New American Standard Bible translate "workmanship" (and that the New International Version translates "handiwork") is *poiema*—from which we get our English word *poem*.

So in a sense that verse is saying that we are God's *poem*—His unique expression of who He is. In the New Living Translation, this is translated as saying we are God's *masterpiece*. Because of this verse, and many more that I teach on in my book *When a Woman Discovers Her Dream,* I believe there is a dream whispered on your daughter's heart. Just as every daddy has a dream for his little girl, our heavenly Father has a dream for each of us too—a dream for how we will shine, bring Him glory, and be His *masterpiece.*

Scripture also instructs us, "Take delight in the LORD, and he will give you the desires of your heart" (Psalm 37:4). God knows what those desires are—and delights in granting them—because He is the one who *plants* those desires in our hearts in the first place as we begin to delight in Him.

How is your daughter God's masterpiece? How can she be His poem, His unique expression of who He is? If she's still young, you have an incredible opportunity to help her discover the dream God has whispered on her heart. And if she's older and still not sure of what God has for her, you still have the privilege of praying about her dream and being there to support her, encourage her, and guide her spiritually no matter what her age.

Ask God for discernment that helps you to see how your daughter is His masterpiece, and He will open your eyes and alert you to the ways He is drawing her into the desires of His heart.

When you begin to believe that every daddy has a dream for his little girl, and God has a dream for your daughter too, you can begin to notice what she does well, ways in which she is unique, and how God might be directing her to be His unique expression of who He is.

Giving Her Permission to Dream

In the Bible, there is a sense in which God gives us permission to dream, and we should give our daughters that permission too.

Philippians 4:13 says: "I can do all this through him who gives me strength."

The Amplified Bible translates that verse like this:

> I have strength for all things in Christ Who empowers me [I am ready for anything and equal to anything through Him

Who infuses inner strength into me; I am self-sufficient in Christ's sufficiency].

And I love how The Message translates that verse: "Whatever I have, wherever I am, I can make it through anything in the One who makes me who I am."

Not only does that verse talk about our ability to live the Christ-directed life and endure anything for His sake, but I believe it also gives us confidence that God will equip us for wherever He calls us.

God is our Dream-Giver, and Ephesians 3:20 describes our Dream-Giver as one who is able to do "*exceedingly abundantly above all that we ask or think,* according to the power that works in us" (NKJV).

The New International Version translates that verse to say God is "able to do *immeasurably more* than all we ask or imagine, according to *his power* that is at work within us."

And finally, The Message puts it this way:

> God can do anything, you know—far more than you could ever imagine or guess or request in your wildest dreams! He does it not by pushing us around but by working within us, his Spirit deeply and gently within us.

We, as moms, can work within our daughters too, gently nudging them toward their God-given dream.

Your Power to Unlock a Dream

I mentioned earlier that some children are dreamers. They dream big and the sky is the limit. But others need encouragement. And they often need that from you. An encouraging teacher who tells your daughter she is capable and can reach the stars, a coach who pulls her—or you—aside and says she has exceptional talent, or you, her mom, looking for ways that she shines and encouraging her in those areas can go a long way in helping your daughter continue to push toward a dream she has.

Beth Hulcy is an example of one young woman who didn't have the teachers or coaches telling her she could excel and reach for the stars. But she had a mom who encouraged her. And that was what it took to propel her to dream big and go for her goals, even though she wasn't a child stand-out or someone who excelled naturally.

"My mom always told me I was smart, even when I struggled in school," Beth said. "She helped me believe that I could do whatever I set my mind to when I remained faithful in prayer. I made it to the University of Okla-homa, joined a sorority, helped start the women's soccer team, gradu-ated, and later obtained two master's degrees. I fulfilled my life dream of becoming a mom, special education teacher, coach, and assistant prin-cipal. Because of her influence, I remember today that I am strong, and because of my walk with Christ, I can do whatever I set my mind to with God's help."

Your daughter may be hearing from lots of people that she has poten-tial. If so, don't underestimate her need to still hear encouraging words from you. And if your daughter is not standing out as exceptionally tal-ented or gifted or capable, all the more reason for her to have you in her corner, like Beth's mom, letting her know she can achieve anything she works toward, anything she puts in God's hands and desires Him to receive the glory for.

I remember my mom typing (on a manual typewriter!) my children's stories and submitting them to book publishing houses for me when I was just eight or nine years old. Even though nothing came to fruition with regard to my writing at that time, my mom's encouragement to me to keep writing and the time she took to send in my work sent a clear sig-nal to me that she believed my writing was worth publishing. She believed in me and my dream.

Our Ability to Crush a Dream

But while we can be on the front lines of helping our daughters achieve their dreams, especially when they are still young and depending on our help, we can also be dream discouragers without realizing it.

There are far too many dream discouragers—and even dream destroy-ers—in this world today. Listen to what they sound like:

- "That's a pretty lofty goal. Why don't you shoot for something more realistic?"

- "The chances of that happening for you are very slim."

- "But you can't really make money doing something like that."

- "That's not a field a Christian should pursue."

- "You could *never* get into that school. They take only the best."

- "You probably aren't smart enough to do something like that."

- "You have to have a lot of money to train for a profession like that."

- "You aren't someone who could succeed in that type of field."

- "That takes a lot of hard work and dedication. I'm not sure you have that in you."

- "It's all about who you know. If you don't know someone in that field, you'll never get in."

I personally heard seven of those ten dream-deterring statements while I was pursuing my journalism degree and later when I was pursuing the publication of my first book. Many people who say the types of things I listed above don't realize they are discouraging someone from dreaming, from trying, from giving it one more shot. And sometimes it is words like those that may cause your daughter to throw in the towel and say, "You're right—how silly of me to think that I could ever do something like that!"

That is why it is so important that you be on the alert for the dream discouragers and the dream destroyers and that *you* be that angel of encouragement in your daughter's life to keep her going when she wonders if she should give up.

Encouraging Her to Dream

Do you know women who have started a hobby or a business, experimented with it a bit, and then moved on to something else? And they have done this so many times it looks like a pattern? We might look at such behavior and conclude they're flaky. We might balk at their entrepreneurial spirit or think they are simply trying to fill a void in their lives. But I wonder if it's because those women were never allowed to try their hand at fulfilling their dreams when they were a child.

How can we possibly know what our dreams are and what we want to do with our lives if we aren't allowed to get a taste of what's out there?

Here are six steps you can take to encourage your daughter as she discovers and pursues her dream:

1. Let Her Explore

Kelly grew up with a critical mother who didn't lavish much praise on her. But she does remember one thing her mother did well.

"She always allowed me to explore, try, and learn. I devoured books, movies, classes, and school stuff. I asked questions and got answers. I was able to go places and do things to learn more about everything around me, to challenge me, and to let me grow. I had the freedom to be me. I could be the little girl in the ruffled dress with shorts underneath. I could watch and play sports and play with dolls. I could be imaginative or serious and oh-so-mature. Now, my mom didn't always respond positively to what I did, but I was allowed to do what I needed to. For that I will always be grateful. Eventually I became comfortable in my own skin because I was given the freedom to explore who God designed me to be."

Help your daughter explore new areas of interest or opportunity. One of them might become the area in which she truly shines.

2. Look and Listen for What Makes Her Heart Sing

I truly believe that each of us has unique abilities and talents and ways to express them. Kay, whose mom never attended any of her softball games, said, "I wish my mom would have taken the time to learn about or invest in my interests and understand what made me tick.

"I think she was of the mind-set that 'everything should be equal,' not realizing some things were important to some of us kids but not to all of us in the same way. This became most evident during the high school years. Different kids have different interests. God made us each unique, with different talents and gifts."

Rebekah Montgomery, an author who has always dreamed big, had a mother who was tuned in to the dreaming hearts of her children. She attributes her own ability to pursue her dreams to her mother's "find a way" influence.

"Everything was always possible with Mom. She was not in any way an obstructionist," Rebekah said. "Even if something was highly unlikely—like when I wanted to grow up to be a mermaid—she encouraged me to think of the ways I could try to accomplish my goal without outright telling me it was impossible or silly. She would ask questions like, 'What do you think you would like about being a mermaid?' and then she would say, 'How can you do that now?' She encouraged us kids to start with little successes when working toward a goal. And when some part of reaching that goal became difficult or tedious, she told us to turn our pursuit into a game—in other words, to pit ourselves against trials or tedium and win over those things by making them fun."

Sometimes we don't see a dream on our daughter's horizon because that dream is still developing. Or, as it was developing, we weren't necessarily looking for it.

Sara says she wishes she had noticed her daughter's dream when Lauren, now 23, was a little girl. "It took me too long to recognize Lauren's strong gravitation toward the arts. I am not artistically gifted, but she is! She writes music and poetry, sings, plays musical instruments, loves photography, and her painting aptitude is amazing! I wish I had seen this in her when she was little."

Jean, a mother of five daughters ages 2–11 whom we met earlier, is aware of how easily each of them could slip through the cracks when it comes to encouraging them in the area of their dreams.

Jean says, "I spend a lot of time with them and try to be a student of *all* of my daughters—understanding who they are, who they are becoming, and what they want to become. By doing that I get an idea of what God's purpose may be in their lives so I can help steer them in His direction."

And Nicole, a single mom of a preteen daughter, said she first noticed her daughter's inclination toward the arts when she insisted on the space—and paper—to be creative.

"When my daughter took a stand at four years old and demanded an entire ream of paper rather than have it doled out to her one sheet at a time, I gave in and let her have the entire ream. From that day forward, I gave her the space and resources to become a 'little artist' as I still call her today."

What is your daughter saying now about what she is interested in?

What is she saying she no longer wants to do? That can give you an idea of where her dream may or may not lie.

3. Let Her Take a Break—or Change Her Mind

Sometimes our children try something but find it's not what they had hoped for or wanted after all. Yes, we need to teach our children commitment and how to stick with a project, activity, or routine. But if she has put effort into the commitment (and hopefully she never signs up for more than a one-year commitment at a time), let her reevaluate it. If she's feeling unsure about it, it's possible she might need time off to get her heart back for it (as was the case with my daughter when it came to giving up cheerleading and piano playing). Sometimes stepping back will allow your daughter to gain different or new skills that prepare her for whatever's next.

Cheri Gregory says this about being made to continue with her piano lessons when her dream was elsewhere: "I wish my mom could have understood how important horseback riding was to me and let me keep up with my lessons, instead of making me stop riding but continue piano. I took 15 years of piano lessons from top instructors and quit, never to play again, after I went to college. It was such a waste, and I was terrible— just terrible—in performance. On the other hand, my riding instructor said I showed exceptional promise, and I've always wondered what my life might have been like if I could have kept doing the one thing I *wanted* to do. I suspect that the physical activity of horseback riding might have kept me from the eating disorder that later almost killed me."

Your daughter may know more than anyone else when it's time to take a break from something and move on to something else. (Or when it's crucial to stick with something that you don't necessarily feel is worth the time, trouble, or money.) Yes, to excel means hard work. But if she is involved in something she truly doesn't enjoy, then it's not for her. Her dream is something she will want to do, no matter what. And if she drops out for a season, she will return to it again—at the right time—if it really is something that is leading her to God's dream for her.

Dana was ready to quit after her second year of piano (and my mom, an accomplished musician, warned me that the third year was the most difficult and that this might happen). So we let her. And it was okay.

Because music was more ingrained in her than we thought, she came back to it when her heart was ready to pursue it out of inspiration, not obligation. This goes hand-in-hand with the next step.

4. Lighten Up

I don't say this to sound harsh—I say it because we, as moms, can sometimes overdo it when it comes to helping our daughter pursue a dream...or pursue something we believe *must* be their dream. When we become our daughters' cheerleader, we can unintentionally get to the point where we are pushing them and conveying to them that it's more important *how* they do than *what* they do. If your daughter is playing soccer and you absolutely love it, but it's not making her heart sing anymore, then let it go. If it was meant for her, she'll come back to it. If not, she'll be glad you understood and let her move on.

5. Live It Out in Front of Her

Monica, who now has children in their teens, says, "My mom has and continues to inspire me to beat the odds and to never give up—not so much in words that she has said, but in the way she lives her life. She has inspired me to never let my fears be bigger than my dreams and to chase after the desires God has placed in my heart. She inspired me growing up to never be a victim of circumstance. No matter what life threw in my path, with God at my side, I was bigger than any of it. I have always felt that aside from God, my mom is my loudest and boldest cheerleader. I love her and the values she instilled in my life. I will be forever thankful to her."

Your daughter needs to see you pursuing your dream and living it out. That is the best way to encourage her to do the same. If you are not living your dream right now, make sure she knows you fully believe that God can accomplish anything in her life that she gives to Him in faith.

6. Let God into the Process

I mentioned earlier that I was a little fearful when Dana expressed an interest in attending an acting school in Hollywood. I was leery of the liberal influence (and in some cases an anti-God influence) she would receive, of the kinds of peers she would have, and an absence of spiritual mentors in her life in that particular environment. But God worked it out. He's the One who made it clear what He wanted her to do; I didn't have to.

If your daughter is leaning in a direction that concerns you, talk to God about it first. Philippians 4:6-7 encourages us in this regard:

> Don't worry about anything; instead, pray about everything. Tell God what you need, and thank him for all he has done. Then you will experience God's peace, which exceeds anything we can understand. His peace will guard your hearts and minds as you live in Christ Jesus (NLT).

Make it a habit to be in prayer about your daughter's dream. God will make a way for her and clear her out of it if she's merely being distracted.

Our Faith Lesson

Lest we unintentionally become dream destroyers, I believe a faith lesson is appropriate here. If we as moms believe in what a big God can do for us, as little and insignificant as we may be, then our daughters will believe it too.

I love the stories in the Old Testament about how God took seemingly insignificant people and did great things through them. I believe it was so He could put Himself on display. God gets more glory by raising up the underdog than by allowing a superhero to shine, for then people realize it was God who accomplished the task, not the person. For example, God took a stuttering man named Moses and raised him up to be a great deliverer of His people. He took a young man named Gideon, who claimed to be of the "weakest" clan of Manasseh and the "least in my family," and turned him into a mighty warrior.[11] He took a humble shepherd boy named David, who was the youngest of eight sons, and turned him into a giant-slayer (literally) and the greatest king who ever ruled Israel. The stories go on and on. *God can do anything, you know—far more than you could ever imagine or guess or request in your wildest dreams!*

Can you, like David, see your God as a big God, able to raise up shepherd boys into giant slayers and kings? As you dream big and hold on to a firm, expanding faith, your daughter will dream big too, and shoot for the stars.

"My Mom Saw My Potential"

Emma Tarr is a talented 16-year-old who isn't quite sure where God wants her and what it is she'd love to do. But she is sure of one thing: Her mom is in her corner, encouraging her to keep dreaming.

"When it comes to pursuing my passions, my mother has not only been supportive, but more than willing to take the initiative. In fact, if it weren't for her, I probably wouldn't have been brave enough to try half the things I've done. When I was very young, my mom was the one who saw my musical potential and signed me up for piano lessons. She pushed me to pursue vocal training (which I'm so grateful for today), and when I showed a slight interest in taking ballet lessons, she researched the possibilities and got me into a community college class. I'm the type of person who is very indecisive and hesitant, so I've needed someone to help push me to take advantage of opportunities. And in that department, my mom has never let me down.

"The future is definitely a grey area for me. The possibility of a performing arts career has always been in the back of my mind, although whether or not I would want to pursue it remains unclear. However, I know that if I ever went that direction, my mom would be more than willing to help me in any way that she could. I've considered taking a year off before I go to college just to try my luck in the industry, but I was hesitant to tell my parents because I wasn't sure how they would react. When I finally did tell my mother, not only did she agree that it might be a wonderful idea, but she even offered to try to find an agent for me so that we could get a jump start. And I got the same reaction from her when I told her that I was considering modeling, at least to raise money for college.

"That's the kind of woman my mother is—the kind who is willing to do whatever it takes to support what I want to do, even when she's already spread thin juggling work and taking care of our home. Even with something like getting an agent—which we didn't know much about—my mom was willing to fully commit to trying simply because she wants me to be able to get what I want from life. She won't let me back down from something just because I'm afraid of what might happen. In that respect, she's exactly the kind of mom that I've needed in my life, and the kind of mom whom I know I will continue to need. And one day, I hope I can be just as influential in my daughter's life as my mother has been in mine."

··············

Because our daughters are not clones of us, they will have their own ideas of what they would like to become. And it may be very different from what you've imagined for her.

Will you trust God with your daughter's dream? Will you lean upon Him if your daughter ends up wanting to pursue something that is fearful or unfamiliar to you? Will you ask for the Lord's eyes when it comes to discerning the dream on your daughter's heart and His wisdom when it comes to encouraging her to live it out?

He's been waiting all her life for her to discover what it is He wants her to do. As you commit to being a "big God believer," you'll help your daughter to become more of a "big dream believer."

Focusing on Your Daughter's Dream

1. What did your daughter love to play or make believe when she was a little girl?

2. What has she talked of wanting to do with her life?

3. Which of the six steps on pages 113–17 do you need to focus on in order to help your daughter pursue her dream?

4. If your daughter is 16 or older, consider a study together of my book *When a Woman Discovers Her Dream*. The two of you can encourage each other as you discover and begin to live out the dream that God has whispered on each of your hearts. (And no, Mom, it's not too late for you to discover the dream God has whispered on *your* heart as well.)

Praying for Your Daughter's Dream

God, thank You for the dreams You have placed within my daughter's heart. Help me to discern which dreams are from You and which ones are clearly not in her best interest. Help me to be a mom who wisely pulls out of her the dreams that may be locked deep inside and help me to be encouraging and affirming in the presence of those dreams. Help me to guard my mouth and my responses so that I never discourage her from something You may have planted in her heart. Equip me with all I need to be her mentor, cheerleader, and confidence-booster as she pursues her dream. And help me constantly point her to You as the One who can accomplish *anything* in and through her life.

Chapter 7

Preparing Her for Life

Point your kids in the right direction—
when they're old they won't be lost.

PROVERBS 22:6 MSG

When Samantha was 12 years old, her parents divorced and she went to live with her father. Unfortunately, she was at that crucial stage where she needed a mom in her life to teach her how to become a young woman.

"When I tried to talk to her about shaving my legs, my mom would say, 'Oh, you don't need to shave. You can do that when you're older.' But all my friends were shaving by then, so I wanted to know how.

"When my mom thought I needed a training bra, she wrapped one up for me and sent it to me for Christmas. Not knowing what was inside the present, I opened it up in front of my brother and my dad, and that was the 'conversation' my mom and I had about wearing bras. There was no conversation. It was just there. And I had to figure it out."

By the time Samantha was an adult, her mom had been married and divorced three times and was then talking of moving in with her new boyfriend. "When I was making plans for my fifth wedding anniversary, I remember being on the phone with my mom and trying to talk her out of moving in with her boyfriend. Somehow the roles seemed reversed at that point.

"I think if I could sum up what's wrong with the relationship between me and my mom, it would be that she's not the mom," Samantha said. "She doesn't understand boundaries. And when I've needed her to be strong, she deferred to me. She didn't think to protect me very often from what I could and couldn't handle emotionally. And when it came to decisions, it was usually her needs that she considered and not mine.

"I'm grateful that God brought people into my life to be mentors for a time—mentors who helped me in ways my mom should have. For example, He provided a coworker who taught me how to put on makeup. But it would've been so much better if my mom had done that."

Because Samantha's mom spent most of her life dealing with her own issues, she never had the time or energy to invest in helping her daughter transition into womanhood. She wasn't there to help her develop wings or prepare her for life.

Teaching Her to Fly

A daughter needs her mom to gently guide her through the transition into womanhood, not just push her over the ledge when she's ready to go out on her own. There comes a time that we as moms need to back off and let our daughters grow up. But first we need to prepare them for life so they can learn how to fly on their own.

And oh, how my husband and I had to teach our baby bird to fly.

Being an only child, and one who never wanted to be far from home, Dana initially didn't want to go away to college. We were baffled by what appeared to be a fear of the unknown. She had always been motivated, and had always appeared quite independent. She had often spoken of going away to college. But when it came time to pick a school, she said she would rather stay at home and attend the junior college or the state university, both just a bicycle ride in either direction from our home. While Hugh and I were all for paying lower tuition fees (which would have been the case if Dana had attended a junior college), we were also holding a sheet of paper that promised $22,000 per year in grants and scholarships—all hers for the taking if she went to a Christian university just over an hour from our home. It was apparent that Baby Bird needed a push out of the nest.

We listened to Dana's reasoning for wanting to stay home and deduced it was mainly fear. We realized she would be without clear direction at the junior college and it would cost more, financially, for her to stay home and attend the state university than to go to the Christian college, live on campus, and receive a better education (in our estimation). We also looked at what the public and the private universities had to offer in terms of her abilities and interests. Finally her father and I made the decision: Baby Bird needed to be nudged out of the nest. It was time she learned to fly.

Hugh sat down with Dana and told her it was time to be bold and exercise her faith in a God who was clearly opening doors for her for something more. He also asked her to trust her parents by trying one year at the Christian university, after which time we would let her decide if she wanted to continue. (We also threw in an offer to pay for her gas if she wanted to drive home the first few weekends if she got too homesick.) After two weeks of prayer that God would give her the confidence to walk through the door we believed He was opening for her, she came home from youth group one evening and announced, "I'm going to trust God and my parents and go away for school."

By God's grace, Dana was assigned a roommate she was very compatible with and they soon became close friends. She found her classes weren't as difficult as she had feared, and she did quite well in them. After just a couple weeks into the semester, she was already planning out her course load for the next three years. After the first semester, Dana ended up on the dean's list, keeping her scholarships and working her way through college by coming home on weekends to lead worship at our church on Sundays. At the time I'm writing this, she is on track to graduate a semester early and is more than ready to soar into what God has for her next. With prayer, guidance, and God's help, Dana developed her wings and learned to fly.

Work Yourself Out of a Job

It is our job, as moms, to prepare our daughters for life. We are to train them to become adults who can stand on their own two feet, support themselves financially, make their own decisions, and succeed in life. I believe we can best do that when we teach them to be less dependent on us and more dependent on God. We will not always be there to guide them through every step in their lives, but God will. We want our daughters calling upon *Him* for help, not calling on us with every decision they need to make. While it's flattering when our adult daughters still want us to be a large part of their lives, our goal should be to help them move on from their dependence on Mother to a mature and confident dependence on their Maker.

Let's consider again Rebekah Montgomery, who comes from a long line of inspiring women. Listen to the resume of generations of mothers before her:

"I am a daughter of an inspiring woman. She was a talented evangelist who gave that up to pastor her flock of eight children. Her grandmother was a circuit court judge before women had the right to vote, and her great-grandmother was a pioneer doctor when women were largely barred from that profession—a regular Dr. Quinn."

So having a mother who prepared her daughter for life is something Rebekah is well acquainted with.

"My mom was always trying to do herself out of a job as a mother," Rebekah said. "Not that she didn't love being a mom; she just wanted us to be able to take care of ourselves. She taught us the skills for life—cooking, cleaning, sewing, running a business, getting along with authority figures, and dealing with mean or angry or critical folks. She said her job was to prepare us to live without her and she frequently reminded us, 'I won't always be around.' She told us that someday we would be on our own and we would need to know how to change the oil in the car or remove grape juice stains from a good blouse. She believed success in life is a lot of little skills mastered and built upon."

To work ourselves out of a job! That is quite a selfless concept when you think about it. Although you have enjoyed being a mom, if you've done your job well, your daughter shouldn't need you by the time she's an adult. And to be a good, effective mom, you need to be okay with that.

Prepare Her for Life

In the Bible, the apostle Paul instructed Titus to teach the "older women" in his congregation to be "reverent in behavior" so that they could "train the young women to love their husbands and children, to be self-controlled, pure, working at home, kind, and submissive to their own husbands, that the word of God may not be reviled" (Titus 2:3-5 ESV). We see in those words to Titus some instructions for us as "older women" and how we can mentor our daughters—the "younger women"—and prepare them for life.

The older women were urged to "live in a way that honors God. They must not slander others or be heavy drinkers" (verse 3 NLT). Their behavior was to be an example to other young women, wives, and mothers. Likewise, you and I as moms are to teach our daughters by example. We are to model to them how to be a woman, wife, and mother who lives a life pleasing to God.

These are the specific areas in which Scripture exhorts us to teach our daughters so they are prepared for life:

Teach Her How to Love Her Husband and Children

I find it interesting that Scripture exhorts the older women (you and me as moms) to *teach* the younger women (our daughters) to love their husbands and children. One would think that loving a husband and child comes naturally for a wife and mother. But Scripture implies it is something we must learn from others who have gone before us. Admit it—there are moments when you don't necessarily want to be kind to your husband. And there are days (especially if your daughter is a teenager) when you don't necessarily want to put your children first. Because selflessness does not come naturally, we need to learn it. Our daughters need to learn that selflessness from us.

Are you modeling to your daughter how she is to love her husband and children someday? If she is unmarried, are you preparing her for life by training her now about what kindness and submission look like in a marriage? By teaching her that God comes first, her husband second, and her children third, you are teaching her the fundamental relationship principle that Christ taught: Love God with all your heart, soul, and mind, and love your neighbor as yourself (see Matthew 22:37-39). If your daughter is married, her closest "neighbor" is the one she sleeps beside. So whether you like him or not, whether he is a believer or not, whether you are glad she had married him or not, teach her to prioritize her husband—even above you! (I will talk more about this in the last chapter of this book.)

Teach Her to Be Self-Controlled and Pure

To teach our daughters to be self-controlled means teaching them to be *Spirit*-controlled when it comes to their behavior and lifestyle. If everything we do, say, and wear says, "I am under the control and influence of the Holy Spirit, not the world and its lusts," then we are showing our daughters how to live discreetly and purely. They may balk at this when they are teenagers, but they will come to appreciate it as God draws their hearts closer to His and as they age and see the importance of biblical values and priorities.

Teaching our daughters to be pure means not only encouraging sexual purity before they marry, but encouraging them to remain sexually pure to their husbands after they say their marriage vows. I've heard many moms say, "She'd be better off without him, so I hope she comes to her senses," and "They never got along all that well, so I don't blame her for leaving him." But if you are to take God's commands concerning marriage seriously, you will seek restoration for your daughter's marriage above anything else, *even* in cases where it looks like there is no hope.

I know these are difficult words to accept. But consider the fact that God has loved us perfectly even when we have committed spiritual adultery (by loving other people and things more than Him), struggled with countless addictions (anything we need in life more than Him), and are even guilty of abuse (constantly refusing to live up to our covenant of obedience and love toward Him). In spite of the ways in which we resist Him or rebel against Him, He still seeks restoration of our relationship with Him. He is a God who heals and restores, regardless. I pray that is your perspective. That way, your daughter will always have someone in her corner when it comes to honoring God in her marriage. A parent's prayers and support of her daughter's marriage is invaluable.

Teach Her How to Care for Her Home

This should go without saying. And yet as moms we can sometimes take care of our children to the point that we never teach them how to take care of themselves.

Brooke, a 30-year-old wife and mother of two young children, said she found herself ill-equipped when she first married, not knowing how to care for her husband and her home: "My mom did everything for me—to a fault," said Brooke. "She did not prepare me for adulthood in the domestic sense. At 18, I had to struggle with learning how to do laundry, cooking, and other basic chores. This was hard on my husband, who had to coach me on homemaking during our first couple of years of marriage."

Brooke's mom, Denise, now sees in hindsight that she should have helped her daughter develop wings: "I never taught my daughter how to do chores of any kind. I always did the housework for her so she could focus on schoolwork, friends, and activities. After she married, her husband let me hear about how I hadn't equipped her in that way!"

Work yourself out of a job so that, in the event that the roles are reversed (which can very well happen as you get older and need your daughter to care for you), your daughter will know exactly what to do.

Teach Her to Be Kind and Submissive to Her Husband

Those who don't know God watch our lives to see how we are different. Does our belief system make a difference in how we live? And in what ways? The apostle Paul knew way back in the first century that people would find fault with Christianity if believing wives were not being kind and submissive to their husbands, whether or not their husbands were believers. That's why Paul stated wives were to be kind and submissive to their own husbands—*"so that no one will malign the word of God"* (Titus 2:5).

Are you teaching your daughter to be a servant of Christ by first being a servant to her husband? Are you teaching her to be kind to others simply because she is a follower of Christ? The "rules" we choose to adopt as believers are not as important as our relationships and what they say to the world about who we trust and in whom we believe.

Now that we've looked at the three areas of instruction mentioned in Titus 2:3-5, I'd like to add more that are based on my discussions and interviews with seasoned moms who are greatly influencing their daughters. Here are some additional ways you can help prepare your daughter for life.

Help Her Overcome Her Fears

When it came time to choose a college, Dana's fear was being too far from home. But eventually she realized that many more opportunities in life awaited her—if she would venture away from home.

Maybe your daughter struggles with fears like talking to adults, speaking publicly, driving, or getting her first job. Cristina, a young mom of a four-year-old, says she wants to model how her stepmom, Chris, helped her develop an independence and overcome fears in her life: "I want to be that support for my daughter," she said. "I want to be able to identify her weaknesses and help her grow. My mom struck a good balance between challenge and support. Given my personality, if she had only challenged me but not shown support, I wouldn't have risen to the challenge. I needed the support and affirmation too."

Chris said, "When Cristina was younger, she was somewhat fearful of things. She was pushed into situations that were uncomfortable. At seven and eight years old, she and her brother were flying on airplanes by themselves, and things like that.

"She also didn't like making phone calls. I would write out for her on paper what she needed to say, instruct her on how to handle a situation, and then I would leave the room. I also expected her to order her own food at a restaurant and speak when spoken to."

"You also prayed me through a lot of fear," Cristina said to her stepmom. "I've called you many times when I've been worried or overwhelmed, and you took time to pray for me."

Second Timothy 1:7 tells us, "God has not given us a spirit of fear and timidity, but of power, love, and self-discipline" (NLT). Any time your daughter is fearful, she needs to be reminded that God can equip her to do all things (Philippians 4:13) and that He will never leave her or forsake her (Hebrews 13:5).

Help Her Deal with Difficulties

Troubles and difficulties are an inevitable part of life. But rather than running to your daughter's assistance every time she has a difficulty, teach her how to handle a crisis on her own—how to grow through her grievances, how to shine in the struggles. Your daughter needs to develop perseverance, an attitude of never giving up, if she is to soar in life. And this character trait will not only help her soar, but make her a legacy in her children's lives as well.

What is your daughter learning from the way you handle life? Do you fall apart when your plans fall through? Do you completely lose it during a crisis? Or do you model strength and perseverance?

Theresa says this about her mom, who became a legacy in her eyes because of her perseverance through the many trials life brought her way: "My mother was an amazing woman. She suffered many things in her life: three miscarriages, two stillborn babies, and she lost my twin sister when the child was three. My mom's bathrobe caught on fire one morning while making breakfast. She ended up in the hospital with third-degree burns over a large part of her body. Incredibly, my three-year-old twin sister was rushed to the hospital with kidney failure and died while my mom was also in the hospital, being treated for her burns. A few years later, my parents' marriage ended in a bitter divorce.

"A few years after that, we were involved in a car accident. My mother suffered a broken back, and despite three surgeries over three months, she was left unable to walk without braces on her legs and a cane or walker. Later on, and up until she died, she was dependent upon a wheelchair to get around.

"There is so much more that I could say about the trials my mom endured throughout her life. Yet what I remember most about her is her perseverance and utter dependence upon God. She never lost faith! Mom never wanted sympathy or pity. One of her favorite sayings, that I still quote to this day, is 'Someone always has it worse.'

"Mom went on to earn her master's degree in education, and she earned it after her accident! She became a champion for the underdog, for those people who might have been considered undesirable or not worthy of friendship. Toward the end of her life, she lived in a government-subsidized apartment building. The couple living down the hall from her had Down syndrome. She considered this couple to be among her closest friends.

"Whenever I start to feel sorry for myself or feel unhappy with my circumstances, I think of Mom. She inspires me to this day, and I share her story with my children often."

Will your daughter be able to handle crises, pain, or difficulty in life because of how she's seen *you* respond? Let her know that a woman needs perseverance to get through life. And then show her what that looks like.

Help Her Establish Her Identity

You can also help your daughter transition into womanhood by affirming her uniqueness, her femininity, and her independence.

Affirm Her Uniqueness

Brooke, whose mom did everything for her as she was growing up, said her mom did know how to instill a confidence and sense of worth in her when she was younger. Brooke knows today, without a doubt, who she is in God's eyes. And she credits her mom for that.

"My mom encouraged me to be one-of-a-kind," she said. "She would drag me to thrift stores to find the rugged jeans and knee-high combat boots that I was dying to have.

"While the other girls were piling on makeup, she never pressured me to wear it until I felt it was needed. If I wanted to color my hair with a streak of blond down the front, she would buy the peroxide. She always seemed proud of me for being unique and standing out, even though it wasn't with expensive things or even by athletic ability. She liked me for my quirkiness, and I felt secure in myself because of that.

"As an adult, I simply don't have time or energy to be 'original' on the outside, but I certainly feel confident in whom the Lord has designed me to be, and I believe my mom encouraged that in her parenting."

Affirm Her Independence

Another way you can prepare your daughter for life is to affirm her independence. While you may want to keep her your "little girl" forever, it is important that you relate to her as an adult once she becomes one.

Dana had some thoughts on this whole idea of letting go of our daughters and treating them as young women, which I initially had a difficult time doing. Dana had to remind me, at times, that she was old enough to take care of herself, order her own meal at a restaurant, eat when she needed to, study when she needed to, and get to bed and get up in the morning when she needed to, without my reminding her or checking up on her. She sometimes had to remind me, too, that she was old enough to know how to make good decisions on her own.

"My mom needs to realize that she raised me the right way to know what I need to do," Dana said. "I will make the right decision, and I am a good listener and I hear the first time when she tells me something. Because I love my mother, I'm going to follow the things she taught me, so if it has to do with relationships or a work decision, she has taught me what I need to know, and now that I'm 20, I can work toward those decisions on my own."

Respecting her privacy and letting her work through her own struggles is important to her too, I learned: "I value that my mom doesn't have to ask everything about my life because she knows that some things are private. She knows that I will tell her what I need to tell her, and knows that if I don't tell her about a problem that I'm going to be able to fix it on my own. I value the fact that she is letting me grow up and experience real-life challenges. She doesn't do everything for me and lets me take care of my own issues, which shows me that she does love me and raised me the right way."

Affirm Her Womanhood

Chris affirms her stepdaughter, Cristina, as a woman by often telling her she is beautiful, both inside and out.

Cristina said this has meant more to her than her stepmom realized. "I've pretty much struggled my whole life with weight issues, and she's always helped me find things that are flattering for my shape and celebrated my curves and my beauty."

Chris said, "I love helping her try on clothes and I love being the runner, saying, 'Try this one, this would look great on you.'"

Cristina added, "I think that's really important. Daughters need to hear from their moms that they're beautiful."

Be in Her Corner

It will be important for your daughter to be able to make her own decisions and stand by them, even when you don't approve. She may experience difficulty in her relationship with her husband if she feels disabled in decision-making until she gets her parents' (or more specifically, her mother's) approval. Once she marries, she needs to leave and cleave to her husband, and respect his decisions or make decisions together with him. Mom, be supportive of your daughter's support of her husband, if nothing else. You may disagree with her. But you can no longer control her. So find a way to be supportive, regardless.

It is also important for you to be in her corner as a way of affirming to her that she can, indeed, make good decisions. If she still needs guidance, be patient, pray her through it, and then look for opportunities to encourage her. This is one of the best ways you can show your daughter you believe in her—standing by choices she makes on her own.

Barbara, a friend of mine who maintains a close relationship with her daughter, Dana, says, "I never want to say no to her nor her children when they need me. I see it as my legacy. When I'm gone, I want them to remember that I was always there for them."

One of the ways she does that, now that her daughter has a family of her own, is to continually be in Dana's corner on decisions she makes. If no one else is behind her, Mom will be, she says.

"When she tells me what she's doing, where she's going, what she's buying, I just say 'That's great,' 'That's awesome,' or something supportive. If she asks what I think, I'll give my opinion. If she ends up doing something different, I don't comment, and I'd never say, 'I told you so' if her decision bombed."

Now, Barbara's advice is in the context of an adult daughter who has already decided what she's going to do. And it has to do with situations where there isn't a moral or biblical absolute. Sometimes you will prefer that your daughter do things differently, or your way, rather than hers. But if she has already decided on her course of action, respect that. Treat her like an adult. And then support her in the same way you would support a girlfriend who shared her decision about something you didn't necessarily agree with.

Guide Her with Integrity

To be in your daughter's corner and support her doesn't necessarily mean being a yes person. If your daughter is interested in something that isn't for her best good (and you've determined this through prayer and seeking godly advice), then God has you in her life for a reason. Use your discernment and speak up.

"If you don't approve of what your daughter is doing, don't ever let her believe it is affecting your love for her," said Janet Thompson, a friend who instructs women around the world on the importance of mentoring, starting with their daughters.

"I let my daughter know what I think, but it stays consistent with what I believe," Janet said.

Janet's daughter, Kim, was interested in a business venture that Janet and her husband didn't feel comfortable with. They believed it would negatively affect their daughter's Christian testimony and determined they wouldn't be able to personally support the venture, monetarily or in prayer. Janet expressed their convictions and told her daughter, "We know this is what you want to do. However, because we do not believe it is God's best choice for you and something you *should* do, we are not going to be able to pray for your success in this endeavor."

It was difficult for Janet to say that to her daughter, but Janet knew she had to be true to her convictions and also be the one person who would tell Kim what she thought, rather than join the many who were going along with her idea but keeping their feelings to themselves because they didn't want to "rock the boat."

About a week later, Kim and her husband came to Janet's house to tell her and her husband that she was not going to pursue that business venture after all. Her mother's prayer and support had become so important to Kim through the years that she realized nothing was worth the time and effort if her mother didn't approve and wouldn't be praying for its success. Kim ended up going with another business venture a few months later that her mother fully supported and prayed for, and that venture ended up doing far better financially than they had hoped the first one would.

That is not a mother's manipulation. Rather, it was a mom's godly influence. And that is a true story of a daughter recognizing the power of her mom's prayers and the importance of having her mom be in her corner in every venture she undertakes.

Don't underestimate your degree of influence. If you feel strongly about something, and you are convinced it is God's leading, and not just your personal preferences, then your daughter needs to hear about it. And she may one day thank you for it. But either way, you will have done what God has put you in her life to do—guide her in the way she should go.

······················· From Her Perspective ·······················

"I Wish She Would Have Been There..."

I asked Samantha, whose story opened this chapter, to reflect on what she missed the most in not having a mom around during those crucial teenage years. I thought her insights would be helpful to any mom in recognizing what is most important to a young woman when it comes to navigating the transition into adulthood. I know, like me, your mom's heart will be touched. And you will be even more determined to be a very present influence in your daughter's life as you help her develop wings and blossom into a woman.

"My parents divorced when I was in middle school and my mother returned to her hometown across the country to be close to her family, leaving me and my brother to be raised by my father. My mother's move led not only to a physical separation, but also a deep emotional separation. While God ultimately provided and continues to provide many women in my life to fill different facets of the void left by my mom, there are certain things that I wish *she* would have been able to provide for me—especially at such a critical time in my life as a young girl headed for adulthood.

"I wish my mom would have been there to teach me about things like makeup, fashion, and how to embrace my own femininity. I wish she had been available to talk about boys and to instill in me a sense of self-worth, regardless of who liked or didn't like me. I wish she could have been my role model to show me how a woman should be treated. I wish she would have been a parent when I needed one and a friend when I needed one, and that she would've been able to sense the difference.

"While I am married to a truly wonderful man who is so much more than I would have even known to ask for, I wish she had cared enough to make sure he was good enough for me, even though I knew he was, and that she cared enough to come to our wedding.

"I wish she would have been there to tell me that people often label creativity as 'weird' and that some of the people most noted for the successful results of their creativity were often called 'weird.'

"I wish she would have helped me understand that not everyone will like me—that when someone doesn't like me it's not always for a reason, that it's not my job to change their mind, and that being disliked doesn't make me less valuable as a person. I wish she had been there to help me understand this rather than leaving me to learn it through years of striving to make everyone around me like me.

"I wish she would have been there to encourage me to assume the best about people and their words and intentions, rather than worry about what negative things people might be thinking about me.

"When my mom left, it seemed like she felt she was relinquishing her right to have a say in my life; I wish she hadn't felt that way. I wish she had given me a sense that I belonged to someone who cared deeply about everything going on in my life, both the milestones and the seemingly inconsequential.

"Ultimately, I wish my mother would've shown me God's unfailing love for me through expressions of her own love for me."

. . . .

If your daughter is still living at home and dependent on you, be careful to be there for her and help her soar. If she is already on her own, pray for ways to continue to affirm her identity, her uniqueness, and her dreams. She was meant to soar. Here's how you can be the wind beneath her wings.

Helping Your Daughter Develop Wings ·······························

1. Ask your daughter what she feels would be most helpful from you in terms of preparing her for whatever lies ahead. If it's high school, college, job applications, marriage, career preparation, or just the next step she needs to take spiritually, offer to be there. Then pray she will be receptive and communicative with you about how you can help.

2. In what areas do you believe your daughter needs the most inspiration, motivation, or preparation? Write a line or two about what you can do to meet her there:

   modeling servanthood

   overcoming her fears

   dealing with difficulties

   establishing her identity

3. Helping your daughter develop wings is all about instilling in her a confidence in God. Tell or text your daughter, at least once a week, that you are praying for her, whether she has asked you to or not. Text a verse, too, to encourage her. (For verses specific to areas your daughter might be struggling with, see the section "Scriptural Encouragement for Your Daughter" on pages 205–14.)

Praying for Her Independence

God, it is Your goal that my daughter no longer be dependent on me, but learn dependence on You. Help me, through every word I say, to be one who builds courage into her and helps her take the next step with You. Thank You that on the days and in the ways I can't be there, You always are. I commit her to Your care and thank You for holding her heart and guiding her ways.

Chapter 8

Choosing Your Battles Well

*The one who has knowledge uses words with restraint,
and whoever has understanding is even-tempered.*

PROVERBS 17:27

I cried the day I discovered my 18-year-old daughter got a tattoo. A *tattoo*! Without me knowing. She didn't have piercings anywhere but on her ears. She avoided pain at all costs. She *hated* needles. So I figured a tattoo would be taboo to her and that subject would never darken our door.

But it did, without a battle. And that was what I found the most difficult.

I had checked her online bank account (which was tied to mine for overdraft purposes and because she had just turned 18), and I didn't recognize the item for which she spent $77. Fearing identity theft, I looked up the Website for the business where the purchase was made and my heart dropped into my stomach. I called her and asked, cautiously, if there was something she wanted to tell me.

She immediately sensed what I was talking about and sounded concerned. "I was going to tell you, but I knew you'd try to talk me out of it."

(Somehow that point didn't make me feel any better.)

"It's really tiny, right behind my ear, in a place where no one can see it."

"Then why get one at all?" I snapped. "Why not just keep that place hidden with nothing on it?"

"It's mostly for me," she said. "It's the word *dream* in my handwriting with a music note as the letter 'd.' It's right behind my ear so that when I get discouraged and people tell me I'll never achieve my dream or to just give it up, I will just hear encouragement in my ear to continue pursuing my dream."

All her life Dana has collected pictures and motivational sayings about pursuing her dream. Partly because she wanted to be an actress or singer, something few people can attain to. And partly because her mother has written a book on pursuing your dream and used her as an example of a woman who is persistent about reaching her dream.

"Do what you love to do," I would always tell her. And a few times I found myself even being, unintentionally, that dream destroyer by saying, "You should focus on an area that might be easier to excel at," or "You should pursue an area in which you can actually make a living."

So it might have actually been *my* words that Dana was defending herself against by tattooing the word *dream* behind her ear. Yet regardless of what I thought about it, there it was—etched above her ear, back on her scalp, where I was hoping no one would see it. As I sat there in my study after our phone conversation, I realized that I had a choice: I could express my disappointment in her for what she had done and let it form a wedge between us and serve as an affirmation to her that her mother doesn't understand her. (And what good would that do because the deed had already been done!) Or I could ponder what she had said to me, express my regret that she didn't feel she could talk to me about it first, and then tell her it sounded like a neat design and I looked forward to seeing it. I chose the latter, of course. I needed to accept it, let it go, and move on. The "shake it off" voice in my head took over: *It's just a tattoo. Get over it!* So I did.

Dana's hesitancy to discuss the tattoo with me was perhaps good insight on her part. Yes, I would've tried to talk her out of it. There might have even been a battle over it. But would there have needed to be?

There are some things that are clearly spelled out in Scripture as sin. Then there are those things that, under the Old Testament law, were culturally forbidden (the pagan nations branded their bodies and God told His people, the Israelites, not to),[12] and then there are things today that young people, in particular, do to express themselves. Some tattoo a picture of Jesus on their shoulder or a verse on their back or a scriptural reference on their wrist as a way of "branding" themselves as belonging to Christ. Others, like my daughter, want something written on themselves as a reminder or a form of motivation. My comment to others who expressed a desire to have a tattoo had always been "Be original. *Nearly everyone* has a tattoo these days. Stand apart from the world and be unique by *not* getting a tattoo!" But Dana's idea of being unique was to have the word *dream* placed behind her ear.

There are more important battles I could fight.

What's Most Important?

One of the wisest pieces of counsel I received as my daughter entered her preteen years was "Choose the hill on which you'll die." In other words, choose your battles wisely. In the context of raising a daughter, that means not everything is worth arguing about. Determine what is most important, and save your strength for *those* battles. That is, choose the hill upon which you'll die, or the one thing worth battling the most about. Otherwise you'll be fighting battles all the time.

Many Christians I know choose their battles carefully when it comes to raising children. It helps to ask these three questions:

1. Is it illegal?
2. Is it immoral?
3. Is it sinful?

My friend Chris, who has raised three children, two of whom are involved in ministry today, said, "If it was illegal, immoral, or unbiblical, we wouldn't allow it. That was the standard. Untidiness isn't included in one of those three areas—it's more of a personal preference. So we never battled about what their rooms looked like."

I have been guilty, over the years, of turning my personal preferences into laws when they should've remained preferences. I wanted Dana's room spotless all the time. Yet she was a child. I wish now that I had relaxed more about that. Today, Dana is so tidy there isn't a thing under her bed. She can't stand a mess. And she even tidies up piles of mail and other things I leave around the house. Does she get on my case today for not being tidier? No. She has realized that tidiness is a personal preference.

I wish I realized that earlier. If I had, there would have been fewer battles over the "slightly out of order" condition of her room.

If what your daughter wants to do falls into the category of being unlawful, immoral, or sinful, it's worth a battle. But I've found that many times the battles we have with our daughters have to do with matters that are not clearly spelled out in Scripture. In fact, many times they're not truly major issues. Quite often the battles are over mere preferences, and when it comes to maintaining an open and trusting relationship with our daughter, certain battles just aren't that important.

Confronting Our Own Fears

When Dana was about 13 years old, a woman came up to me after church, in front of Dana, and asked, "How can you let your daughter wear makeup? My daughter is only 12 and wants to wear makeup, and I tell her, 'Not until you're 16.' And she says, 'The pastor's wife lets *her* daughter wear makeup and she's not 16 yet, so why can't I?'"

I wish this woman had pulled me aside to have a *private* conversation about this with me. She chose, instead, to present this question right in front of my daughter, who disliked—as any teenager would—the idea of being singled out as "an example" for her peers and parents of peers. Just because Dana's father was the pastor of the church didn't mean Dana should be the "measuring stick" other parents or kids used to determine what they should or shouldn't do. I long feared that Dana might feel this pressure, and here was this woman confirming that Dana did, in fact, live in a fishbowl. I realized my answer—my defense of my daughter or my caving in to the pressure of this woman—could have either an affirming or disparaging impact on my daughter's life. So I breathed a missile prayer—*Help me, Lord*—and stated, firmly but gently, that I have had to choose my battles carefully, and the matter of my daughter wearing a little bit of makeup at the age of 13 wasn't worth a battle in my home.

I added that for Dana to wear makeup before the age of 16 wasn't illegal, immoral, or sinful. Rather, it was a personal preference. And when our daughters reach a certain age at which they want to feel like a young woman and wear a little makeup, that is perhaps when we should be their helpers and advisers rather than their critics.

This mother was adamant, however, that I not "give in" because it was making it harder for her to hold her ground with her own daughter.

"If my daughter starts wearing makeup, then the boys will start calling her, and next she'll want to start dating," she said to me, nearly in tears. I was surprised at what an emotional reaction she was having over the request to wear a little mascara. This poor mom was unaware that her daughter was probably already talking to boys at school and at church, and that if she wasn't allowed to do certain things in her own home, she might try to find a way anyway. This mother had fears, I could see, and was afraid that her daughter was growing up too quickly.

I assured this mom that it's natural for a young girl (even at age 12) to want to do things that will make her feel more attractive as a young woman. I suggested she take her daughter to a department store cosmetics counter and have a "makeover" *with* her so the two of them could learn about modest makeup application and she could take part in the experience with her daughter as a way of supporting her, giving guidance as to how much is too much, and understanding the need her daughter felt in wanting to wear makeup like other girls her age. I suggested that it could be a bonding experience between the two of them and not to underestimate how much something like that would mean to her daughter, who probably already felt her mother didn't understand her or support her.

Anticipate Her Needs

In all fairness, I have witnessed my own fears come into play the first time Dana applied heavy eyeliner (that was just a brief phase, thank the Lord!), when a boy I didn't know started texting my daughter, when phone calls started taking place before I knew who she was talking to, and when she wanted to go on a group date to the movies with friends. When those situations came upon us, I realized I was a little late in anticipating them and making sure I discussed them with her ahead of time so she would know exactly what was important to us and what we expected of her. Looking back now, I tended to panic—and overreact (much like that mom who approached me at church!)—because I was caught off guard. I felt I had to catch up to the situation with thrown-together rules and standards off the top of my head. That was nerve-racking and confusing for

Dana and for me. And, again, as I look back at what happened, it was my own fears that I needed to confront, not Dana's trustworthiness.

Shea says, in retrospect, that she wished her mom had anticipated her needs when she was a teenager: "I realize my mom had her hands full being a single parent to two teenagers," she said. "I'm sure some days she was doing good to just keep her head above water. I know she did her best, but during my teen years, my mom was a bit out of touch with happenings at school, what problems teenage girls of my generation were facing, and issues I needed to be educated on.

"Like I said, she did the best she could, but I was misinformed on a lot of topics because I simply just went with what I was told by other kids at school. Educating herself and being proactive in talking with me would have gone a long way, instead of me waiting until I was already in a bad situation and ended up having to go to her for help."

Ingredients for the Battle

After interviewing many young women and their mothers, and having experienced my own share of unwarranted battles with my daughter, I identified the ingredients that often brew into a battle. These are the factors that can contribute to unnecessary drama with your daughter, depending on her age and the situation. Be aware of them, and you may be able to avoid some unnecessary battles.

Generational Differences

Christi, the mom of a 15-year-old, says, "My daughter doesn't seem to listen to my advice anymore. In fact, she makes it clear that 'things are different now,' so my insight, experience, and wisdom don't appear to be important or necessary to her."

My daughter can tend to agree: "Some of the differences between moms and daughters are accentuated by our different generations. Our culture today is different, our technology is different, and our clothes are different. We are going to be different from our mothers simply because we live in a different era. So it's difficult when mothers want their daughters to do everything they did when they were in high school or dress and act the same way when things are just naturally different."

For years, Dana laughed at how "high" I wore my pants. To the contrary, I balked at how "low" the pants were on girls her age. To me, it seemed immodest. To her, the high-waisted pants seemed ridiculous (until they came back into fashion a few years later, and *then* she wore them!). Different isn't necessarily wrong. Same goes with how your daughter raises her children now or someday, how she chooses to discipline them, and how she and her husband run their household. Your daughter will do many things differently than you did. But don't let that generational difference be cause for a battle or a rift in your relationship. Instead, pray for discernment and an open mind to understand and appreciate your daughter as a woman in a different generation.

When you understand—and appreciate—that there will naturally be differences in your preferences, and you're okay with that, your daughter will want to talk more openly with you about what she is thinking, how she'd like to change her hair, why certain clothing is important to her, and so on. Be approachable by considering that she lives in a different generation and what seemed "right" to you might not necessarily be right or wrong, it just might be what's most familiar and comfortable to your generation—but not hers.

Personality Differences

We will differ from our daughters not only because of our age and our generation, but also because of our personalities and the way we receive from and respond to one another. Kelly says this about her mom, with whom she makes a conscious effort to emotionally connect: "My mom is very conscious about and interested in the world around her. She is very current with world news, politics, and local news as well. I value her desire to learn and participate. She rubbed off on me and I am also very interested in these areas. We can have in-depth and long conversations regarding our world. However, they can become contentious if she feels I disagree with her. Disagreement equals dislike in her world."

Because Kelly loves the times she can evaluate and discuss things with her mother, she says she tries "very hard to be respectful and open. I watch my words and actions carefully."

Does your daughter walk on eggshells around you because of your different personalities, different ways of approaching or expressing things, or your different ways of receiving from, interpreting, or responding to each other? Maybe you are the one who walks on eggshells around her. Keep in mind your own personality quirks and how you respond, and that may help keep the otherwise enjoyable times from turning into battles.

Lack of Trust

I regretfully admit that I had a difficult time trusting Dana. But it wasn't because Dana proved herself untrustworthy. It was because I remembered what I was capable of doing and lying about and getting away with as a teenager. I was a pretty well-behaved teenager who never got into serious trouble, but I did know how to pull something over on my parents or stretch the rules or justify a compromise in my mind. Because of that, I didn't want to be the naive mom on the other side of a possible lie. But treating Dana according to what I believed she was *capable* of, as opposed to who she really was, wasn't fair to her.

I often remember Dana saying, "You don't trust me." And I remember responding with, "Yes, I trust you, Dana, but I don't necessarily trust those you are with." Or, I made some other excuse for not giving her the trust or freedom she had earned. Looking back now, I assumed the worst at times because I was expecting her to act like a "typical" teenager— deceitful, aloof, irresponsible, forgetful, discourteous, and so on. But that wasn't the teenager I had. I wish now that I had looked at who my daughter was and trusted her and how we had raised her and not been so insecure about what "might" happen.

"Just because my mom may have made certain mistakes when she was young doesn't mean I will make those same mistakes," Dana said. "I need her to trust me by knowing that I have learned from the mistakes she has shared with me, and I will strive for excellence because I want to make her proud of me."

Apparently I was not alone in my unwarranted hesitancy to trust my daughter. Annie, a friend of Dana's, had similar thoughts: "My mom should've allowed for a bit more freedom when I was beginning high school. She didn't trust me even though she didn't have a reason not to trust me. I think that made me want to be rebellious too. Because my parents were so focused on everything I was doing or not doing it made me think, *Maybe I should really give them something to worry about if they're going to worry like that anyway.*"

Don't give your daughter a reason for you to mistrust her. Give her the benefit of the doubt. You want her to expect the best in you. *You* expect the best in *her*.

Inconsistency

An inconsistency in our rules or lifestyle can cause a battle that we will surely lose. If your daughter sees you doing something she's not allowed to do, you may hear about it. Some situations she'll have to deal with (such as "Why can't I drive?" if she doesn't have a license or "Why can't I drink?" if she's underage). Other situations, *you* may have to deal with.

When we started telling our daughter she had to go upstairs and couldn't watch certain movies that my husband and I decided to watch because they were inappropriate for her age, I realized that some of the movies weren't appropriate for *any* age. At least, that was my *personal* conviction. It was then that I decided, if it wasn't emotionally or spiritually healthy for her, it wasn't healthy for me either. Most of what I didn't want her to see had excessive violence, sexual inappropriateness, or foul language. Regardless of my age, that content isn't good for my soul and spirit either. The day I became consistent in my standards for her and for me, too, was the day I found freedom (from the guilt of feeling I had double standards as well as the sorrow of having to exclude her from something so I could feel like a "responsible" parent).

And now that Dana is an adult, I have noticed that, for the most part, whatever I don't care to watch or read or spend my time on, she doesn't care to watch or read either, even though she is old enough to decide for herself what she'd like in the area of entertainment. That is influence that happened without me realizing it. I was simply trying to be consistent with my own heart. And I believe that God honored it with the convictions that Dana now holds.

Inconsistency can cover a broad range of issues. Some moms found it led to a battle when they were inconsistent with the rules between an older daughter and a younger daughter, or with the standards they set forth for their son as opposed to their daughter. Our children notice when we don't hold to a standard that we set, or when we raise that standard for them, but not for their sibling. Aim to be consistent in all areas of life, and you will likely minimize the battles on the home front.

Hormonal Clashes

Is there any other way to say it? Take a hormonal teenager and a mom going through premenopause and it can spell complete chaos. Today, Dana and I have to laugh when we hear ourselves being absolutely unreasonable with each other. It's often because we are both on the same hormonal cycle or we're at clashing extremes in the hormonal spectrum. Now this can't be an excuse. Sometimes, one of our hearts—or both of them— simply aren't right before God, causing us to be selfish, impatient, or irritated with each other. In situations like this, don't overreact, don't lose your cool, and, as said earlier, don't assume the worst.

What God Values

What battles, then, should we choose? Which issues are worth fighting for? The ones closest to God's heart.

Remember that God loves your daughter even more than you do. And His desire for her is the same as His desire for you: "that you may live a life worthy of the Lord and please him in every way: bearing fruit in every good work, growing in the knowledge of God, being strengthened with all power according to his glorious might so that you may have great endurance and patience" (Colossians 1:10-11).

So, as *you* seek to become all that God desires of you, pray for the wisdom to guide your daughter, regardless of her age, into the woman God desires her to be. Times of discipline, exhortation, heart-to-heart talks, or explanation are key moments that we can influence our daughters in what is most important to God's heart and, therefore, to ours. But to incorporate this kind of spiritual wisdom during times when we are laying down the law or seeking to provide consequences for their disobedience, or letting them know when we disapprove of their actions, we need to realize that God is more concerned with her heart than her hair color. He cares more about her degree of compassion than her chosen degree or career. He is more concerned with her ability to encourage than to excel. He wants her to gain wisdom, not necessarily win trophies.

As *you* focus on what is most important to God, you can focus less on the small stuff when it comes to your daughter. And as you focus on what God wants of her, it will be a constant reminder to you of what God wants of *you* as well. Let's look now at what Scripture points out as being most important to God's heart.

Loving God and Others Above All Else

When a man asked Jesus which of the commandments of God was the greatest, Jesus replied:

> "'You shall love the Lord your God with all your heart, and with all your soul, and with all your mind.' This is the great and foremost commandment. The second is like it, 'You shall love your neighbor as yourself.' On these two command-ments depend the whole Law and the Prophets" (Matthew 22:37-40 NASB).

By asking Jesus which commandment was the greatest, the man was really asking, "Which of the many commandments should I focus on?" I think we can ask that when it comes to which battles are most impor-tant too.

When an issue comes up with your daughter that has at stake the issue of loving God and others, it is one worth fighting for. I know moms who have had clothing discussions with their daughter centered around what it really means to love God first and love others (and therefore not tease them or provoke them) by what we wear. I have had discussions with my daughter about what it really means to love God and others when it came to including other kids, or putting up with personalities she would rather avoid, or extending herself to others in her youth group, when she'd rather stay at home or go to a different one that was more "popu-lar" across town. When we model a love for God and others in our lives, we can more easily show our daughters how important it is that their thoughts, words, choices, and actions show a love for God first, and then a love for others.

Becoming Christlike in Every Area of Life

The amount of instruction in the New Testament that teaches us to become more like Christ attests to the fact that it is an important issue with God. He wants us to be "conformed to the image of his Son" (Romans 8:29) and "transformed" by the renewing of our minds (Romans 12:2) and "crucified with Christ" so that we are not the ones who live, but Christ lives in us (Galatians 2:20). By running your daughter's requests, choices, words, and attitudes through the grid of Christlikeness, you can not only better choose what battles are worth fighting, but you can also constantly reinforce to her what matters most. If every decision comes down to the question of whether or not it mirrors Christ's behavior, then we no longer have battles with our daughters, we have mentoring moments with them.

Again, this is where it is so important that you and I live out the example before our daughters. We can tell them all our lives that they need to be more like Christ, but they will model their lives after what they see in front of them—by what they see in us. Are they seeing you "live a life worthy of the Lord" by pleasing Him in every way and "bearing fruit in every good work" (Colossians 1:10)?

If so, then you can run her actions, and yours, through the grid of the fruit of the Spirit in Galatians 5:22-23:

Is this word, choice, or action loving?

Is it going to produce joy?

Will it result in peace?

Is it showing patience?

Is it full of kindness?

Does it embody goodness?

Does it exhibit faithfulness?

Does it show gentleness?

Does it display self-control?

Not only can you run her requests (and your rules) through that filter, but you can also run your responses to her through that filter as well.

Be familiar with the fruit of the Spirit (love, joy, peace, patience, kindness, goodness, faithfulness, gentleness, and self-control), and keep that list in front of you when it comes to guiding your daughter's attitudes and actions. The great thing about keeping that list in front of us is that it reminds us of the manner in which we should respond toward their attitudes and actions. We need to make sure we respond to our daughters with love, peace, patience, kindness, and so on.

Becoming a Person of Gratitude

One of the attitudes that we, as moms, cannot ignore is the degree of gratitude that is—or is not—expressed by our daughters. Is she displaying ingratitude? Is she taking her blessings for granted? Is she constantly complaining?

God's Word says, "In everything give thanks; for *this is God's will for you* in Christ Jesus" (1 Thessalonians 5:18 NASB). God's will is that our daughters become women who are thankful in all things. He desires that we—and our daughters—become people of praise who constantly thank, not continually criticize. Are you a woman who is modeling thankfulness to your child or grown daughter? Be that woman you want her to be as well. Be a mom who is thankful in all things.

Diffusing the Battle

So how can you diffuse a battle that may be brewing because of those generational or personality differences or the hormonal clashes? By being aware of the ingredients for battle and focusing on the areas God says are most important. Then keep in mind the following principles:

1. Don't Overreact

Sometimes it is easy to think the worst and overreact to a situation, and to draw a conclusion that is based on too little information. To react emotionally, rather than rationally and maturely, tends to escalate a discussion into a battle. This is where James 1:19 is so appropriate for us as moms, especially in the heat of the battle: "Everyone should be quick to listen, slow to speak and slow to become angry; because human anger does not produce the righteousness that God desires."

2. Don't Lose Your Cool

Our volume and energy level can greatly escalate or eliminate a battle in the making. After many times of completely blowing it in this area, I have learned to say a quick prayer in the heat of the moment: "God, give me wisdom to respond in a way that will bring about a gentle and loving response from her." When I put the emotional thermometer in my lap and make it *my* responsibility, it's amazing how much that can help diffuse or eliminate a battle altogether.

Cheryl—mom of a now-17-year-old daughter, Kaylee, who came to live with her as a foster child when she was 13—has had her share of moments when she's lost her cool. But, she says, it is healthy when it's a private situation with you and your God.

"Allow the meltdowns to happen—hers *and* yours! Pent-up emotions aren't ever good. But, have your meltdown in private—laying it all at Jesus' feet. Good things can happen (in terms of repentance, God working on your heart and hers, and restoration of the relationship) in the wake of a meltdown."

3. Don't Let Your Pride Get in the Way

It seems like Dana and I went through a "fighting all the time" phase during her early teen years because I wasn't choosing my battles wisely. Some battles were because I was afraid of how something would "look" and I was (oh how I hate to admit this!) afraid of how it would make *me* look. That is pride. And my pride is *not* justification for a battle. Because pride issues are often rooted in legalism, I want to close out this chapter by addressing this topic that might be closer to our hearts than we'd like to admit.

Lose the Legalism

As a Christian parent, and having been raised by Christian parents (as well as being a pastor's wife for nearly 25 years), I have witnessed many potential and full-fledged wars fought on the battlefield of legalism—that place where we, as parents, have certain rules based on tradition or preference or pride, rather than on Scripture. Robert Jeffress, in his book *Grace Gone Wild*, says legalism is "obedience to the wrong standard for the wrong reasons."

"Legalists constantly add to the Bible's standards of conduct for Christians. They tend to place Christians under a code of conduct that is either based on antiquated Jewish laws that are not applicable to Christians today or on the opinions and prejudices of others."[13] He goes on to say that a great definition of legalism is "forcing my opinion to become your conviction."[14] Legalism in your parenting can kill the heart of your daughter. It can also drive her away from your faith.

Moms, it is in our nature as human beings to be focused on how things look rather than how things are. We can tend to be more concerned with others' opinions than with God's, more focused on the rules rather than the relationship between us and our daughters. I want to be a mom who holds to God's standard for me and my daughter—not the standard everyone else thinks I should hold for her or myself. I want to be a mom who sees my daughter through eyes of grace, not eyes of condemnation. I can be a mom who doesn't worry about things that don't truly matter in the long run when I am focused more on her heart than her hair color, on her individuality, not my own image. That is easier to do when I am grounded in God's Word (and what it does and doesn't say) and am ever reminded of the love and grace He has extended toward me.

I need to live day to day ever aware that I have sinned and fallen short of the glory of God (Romans 3:23), and that I have disappointed God as many times, if not more, than my daughter has disappointed me. When I am aware of my own inability at times to meet God's standards, I can extend more grace to my daughter, who may be unable, at times, to meet *my* standards. To extend grace to our daughters doesn't mean we excuse or ignore their ungodly behavior. It means we extend to them the same undeserved favor that we didn't deserve from God, yet He extended to us.

I regret my earlier years as a mother when I was very judgmental, an action that was rooted in legalism, not love. I wish now I had been quicker to extend grace rather than quick to criticize. In an effort to show my daughter what was modest, upright, and biblical, I cut down others whom I believed weren't. And by doing so, I showed my daughter I was a critical person rather than a compassionate and gracious one. My daughter will see biblical values by what she sees in *me*, not in what she hears or sees me point out in others. She will learn modesty by how I dress, not by how I point the finger at others dressed inappropriately. She will know what it means to love God and others above all else, live Christlike in every area of life, and be a woman of gratitude by what she sees in *my* life. So, like it or not, you and I are the ones on display.

Dear mother, for your daughter's sake, be a woman (like I am striving to be) who expresses compassion, not criticism, and who exhibits love rather than legalism. It will show. And it will speak louder than your lectures.

As I wrote that paragraph above, I thought about a brief conversation I had yesterday with my daughter. We were sitting at the mall when she showed me a picture of a friend of hers who is still struggling with living a God-honoring lifestyle. Her perspective, although she didn't say it verbally, was "Here's my friend, the one I'm still praying for." But *my* perspective (and shame on me for saying it verbally) was "There's that guy who is still living in sin."

Dana never rolled her eyes at me. She never raised her voice. She just lowered her eyes, sighed softly, and said, "I choose to not judge him." We talked about God being the One who calls things right and wrong and how important it is for us to not tolerate what God clearly calls sin. But in the discussion we had, I can see more clearly today that Dana is the one who displayed God's love and I am the one who displayed legalism. She saw that boy for who he was. I saw him for what he was doing. She was expressing hope that he would come around. I already had him condemned. In the quiet moments as I write this, I have confessed my heart to God and asked for the ability to see others through His eyes.

Just minutes ago, I sent Dana a text message that said, "I'm glad [this young man] has a good friend like you who loves him as God does. I'm writing a chapter on extending grace, and I am realizing that you showed it far better than I did."

Dana's gracious response was simply: "Thanks! ☺"

Finding the Balance

Moms, I encourage you to pray for a heart like Jesus' when it comes to sin in your daughter's or anyone else's life. We will avoid battles with our daughters, throughout their lives, if we learn the healthy balance between hating the sin but loving the sinner. And may God give us grace to abhor the sin in our own lives while we strive to be obedient to Him, yet keep our arms and hearts open to our daughters and others who are striving— or struggling—themselves.

Keep in mind God's grace when you draw the boundaries and set the standards in your home. Be careful to not call something God's law if it isn't. As 1 Corinthians 10:23 says, "All things are lawful, but not all things are profitable. All things are lawful, but not all things edify" (NASB). In other words, as those who are in Christ, we are free to do *anything* that does not contradict the laws of God. But we should only do what is *helpful* to us and others in their walk with God. That may mean letting go of certain preferences for the sake of others.

In The Message, 1 Corinthians 10:23 reads like this:

> Looking at it one way, you could say, "Anything goes. Because of God's immense generosity and grace, we don't have to dissect and scrutinize every action to see if it will pass muster." But the point is not to just get by. We want to live well, but our foremost efforts should be to help *others* live well.

That is a loving attitude toward life, not a legalistic one. I have known many Christian parents who have done more harm than good by making rules where there aren't any. They have, although unintentionally, taken their children's freedom in Christ and tried to bind them with their own traditions and rules. I have learned that I can't make my daughter abide by such rules. It wouldn't be fair or loving.

I want my daughter to understand she is free in Christ—that all things are lawful for her, but not all things are profitable. So far, she's done just beautifully when it comes to making choices that will honor God (and no, I don't hold the tattoo incident against her—and hope you won't either!). She has said no to quite a few situations in her life—not because they were wrong or sinful, but because as a leader at her school and church, she has chosen not to risk offending or causing another to stumble in any way.

There are some things Dana has chosen not to do simply because we frown upon them. And there are decisions she makes, as a young woman, because the Holy Spirit is at work in her life as well. Allow the Holy Spirit the chance to develop convictions in your daughter—even if sometimes they are different than yours—and trust His work in her life.

"I Needed Her to Trust Me"

At a very young age, Tracie had a heart to be obedient. But she needed her mom to trust her heart and not be so worried she would cross the line or rebel. Listen to the heart of this daughter whose greatest need was—and still is—to be trusted.

"My mom did a great job of providing structure and boundaries, and she was loving and showered me with attention...but maybe a little too much! I did not have much independence or freedom to make my own decisions. I was a good girl so I did not need much in the way of discipline; I was already extremely conscious of right and wrong and was constantly trying to meet God's high standards.

"While my mom seemed to understand my own high standards, she nevertheless was hard on me. It often seemed that her standards were even higher than God's! The more formative behavior, however, was that her concern that I avoid mistakes and walk the straight and narrow meant that she sheltered me and tried to keep me a little girl for as long as she could. This did not do me any favors as I moved into my teen years. It also contributed to my disillusionment with the 'Christian world' when I moved into college (and a Christian college at that!). I spent a good many years trying to reconcile the church and the world. The greatest impact was a feeling that I had no control over my life. This came out in some negative ways in my later years."

Today, Tracie says she has a very close relationship with her mom.

"I am an adult now, and thankfully, my mom has turned out to be an excellent listener. I truly can tell her anything—and have. I went through a period in my life of great struggle and falling away from the Lord. Having spent the first thirty-plus years of my life living or aspiring to live a godly life, I finally went through the rebellion that I never experienced in my teens or college years. My experimentation with worldly pursuits led to a worldly lifestyle—men, drinking, and a host of other unholy activities and habits.

"Through it all, my mom listened to me and never passed judgment. She was quiet when I needed it and offered advice and wisdom when I needed it. I respect her greatly for her restraint—I can only imagine all the things she wanted to say!—and for her constant love and acceptance. Through it all, I have been able to say anything, knowing she would always be there for me. As I've shifted my focus from the world back to the Lord, I can see just how great her influence has been on my life. God used her patience and mercy in ways she probably will never know."

⋯⋯⋯⋯⋯⋯⋯

Aren't you relieved that God sees your heart and that you are not out on that battlefield alone? In fact, most of the battles God wins in the hearts of our daughters are fought on our knees, in prayer. I love the words of Moses to God's people as they were caught between the Egyptian army and the Red Sea. Just before God parted the sea and let the people walk through the seabed on dry land and closed it up on their enemies, Moses said, "The Lord will fight for you; you need only to be still" (Exodus 14:14). In the NASB that verse says, "The Lord will fight for you while you keep silent." And I especially love the blunt, practical translation of that verse in The Message: "GOD will fight the battle for you. And you? You keep your mouths shut!"

Sometimes instead of talking to our children about God, we must talk to God about our children. Sometimes instead of crying or complaining to our daughters about their choices, lifestyle, or attitudes, crying out to God does far more good.

Sometimes the *only* thing you can do is pray. But you can always be assured it is the most effective thing you can do. Don't turn to prayer as a last resort! Pray for wisdom to choose your battles wisely. Pray for love so you don't fall into the trap of imposing legalism. And pray for words that speak gently but firmly about the convictions on your heart.

A Reassessment of the Battle ··

1. As you think about the most recent—or most pressing—battle between you and your daughter, ask yourself: Was her action or intention illegal, immoral, or sinful? If not, it might be a situation in which you need to revisit the topic with trust in her and what you have taught her.

2. What is one way you can…

   Be more understanding of the generational differences between the two of you?

   Be more understanding of the personality differences between the two of you?

   Extend trust to her in a situation where she has proven herself?

   Provide consistency in your lifestyle with what you are expecting of her?

3. What insights do the following verses offer when it comes to diffusing or eliminating a battle with your daughter?

Proverbs 15:1:

1 Corinthians 13:4:

Galatians 5:22-23:

Ephesians 4:2:

Philippians 2:2:

James 1:19-20:

1 Peter 4:8:

A Prayer for Peace

Lord, I realize anger does not accomplish the righteousness of God. Yet there are times I can become angry, frustrated, and at wit's end with my daughter. During those times, let me see her through Your eyes and remember that You have given me the assignment of raising her to love and honor You. Give me the wisdom to choose my battles wisely, to rule her in love and not through legalism, to keep my cool and protect her heart as I discipline her in love. Help me to trust her in the areas where she has earned my trust and to trust You with the things I cannot control. I pray for peace to rule over our relationship...in Jesus' name.

Chapter 9

Guiding Her Spiritually

*(Love) bears all things, believes all things, hopes all
things, endures all things. Love never fails...*

1 Corinthians 13:7-8 nkjv

"My daughter always said she wanted to grow up to be just like me,"
Janet told me as we sat together for dinner. But Janet assumed the
person Kim wanted to imitate was the Janet who, in her forties, recommitted her life to Christ and turned from her rebellious ways, and started
living the way God wanted her to. But when Kim was a young teenager,
Janet heard her saying, "I want to go to college, get married, have a baby,
get a divorce, have a career, and then live with my boyfriend."

Janet was shocked to hear her daughter recount every step *she* had
taken before she knew Christ. She was hoping Kim, by then, would have
learned from her mother's mistakes and want to imitate the *right* choices
she had seen her mother make more recently.

Sure enough, when Kim turned 18 years old, she started repeating her
mother's mistakes. Janet had originally anticipated that year would hold
fun shopping trips, buying necessities for Kim's college dorm room, and
helping her settle into her first home away from home. Instead, she found
herself sobbing in her driveway as her daughter drove away with her car
packed up and her mind made up about moving in with her boyfriend.

"Kim had always said she wanted to be just like me," Janet wrote in her
book *Praying for Your Prodigal Daughter.* "I was sure that just as she had
imitated my wayward behavior, she would follow suit when I rededicated
my life to the Lord, married a godly man, and enjoyed a Christ-centered

marriage and home. But she didn't. Instead, Kim was angry and confused at my new Christian life and wanted no part of it."[15]

In her book, Janet details the journey of praying for her daughter daily for five years. Three years later, Janet received the long-awaited call. Kim was leaving her boyfriend and asked if she could return home and look for work. She still wasn't ready to live a Christian life, so Janet continued praying for her daughter's salvation and for her to find a godly man and a job in a small, family-owned business that would treat her well in her first career position.

After several interviews, Kim received a job offer at a local, family-owned wholesale nursery, where she met a man named Toby and fell in love. Janet was disappointed and confused because she had been praying for the past four years that her daughter would marry a godly man, and Toby wasn't a believer at the time. So when Toby asked for Kim's hand in marriage, Janet showed him her devotional prayer journal and explained she'd been praying for a godly man to come into her daughter's life and she wasn't sure he was the one.

But because of her prayers, Janet was trusting that God had a plan. As an engagement gift, she and her husband gave Kim and her fiancé a biblically based premarital counseling course. God answered her prayers as both Kim and Toby surrendered their hearts to Christ and made a commitment to live Christ-centered lives. At last, her prodigal daughter had come home! Just short of five years after beginning to pray for her daughter's salvation, Janet saw her daughter make a public profession of faith through baptism. And a couple weeks later, Kim married her godly man, Toby.

In retrospect, Janet says, we must be the kind of women we are striving for our daughters to become.

"Women so often want to influence others, mentor others, and have a ministry that makes a difference in people's lives," said Janet, founder of About His Work Ministries, and author of several books on mentoring. "But the first person you should be mentoring and directing is your own child.

"Do you have the walk with God that you want your daughter to have? Do you have the marriage you want your daughter to have?"

To guide your daughter spiritually and raise her into a godly woman, you must *be* that godly woman you strive for her to become.

Your Role in Her Life

If later in life you became a Christian, or like Janet recommitted your life to the Lord and are now hoping to instill Christlike values in your daughter, it's never too late to start. Or, if you raised your daughter to be a believer and you still want to do everything you can to guide her spiritually, I'm glad you are realizing your job isn't yet done.

We can prayerfully be a spiritual influence on our daughters all our lives, helping them draw closer to the Lord as they see us reflecting Christlike behavior. That is where we will focus in this chapter—on how *you* can be the woman you want your daughter to become. Because you are her mom, she will always look to you for love, acceptance, and affirmation. And you want to make it possible for her (if she hasn't already) to look to you as her spiritual mentor too.

I have interviewed several seasoned moms who have been a godly influence on their daughters, who have inspired them to ministry or helped them become the godly wives and mothers they are today. And in the upcoming pages, I'll share their wisdom and advice about how to guide your daughter spiritually no matter how young or old she is.

No Backing Down

The most obvious behavior I saw in godly mothers of godly daughters is that those moms never backed down. Believing in their God was not optional for their daughters. Neither was it obligatory. It was a way of life. It was the *only* way to live. A godly woman never backs down when it comes to her children's salvation.

Stella's mom, Matilda, is now 87 years old. She raised her children to love, obey, and serve God, and she is seeing the fruit of her labor: four generations of children in ministry. Stella shares the secret behind her mom's inspiration.

"Mom believed a relationship with God was the most important aspect of her children's lives," Stella said. "When she heard the Word, she shared it with us. As teenagers, we all gave our life to Christ, and now Mom's legacy has been going on and on."

Stella, her three sisters, and her brother are all involved in ministry, as are her children and her sibling's children and *their* children as well.

"Some moms don't want to push their faith on their kids, yet Mom's opinion was 'Why wouldn't you push medication on your child if she was sick?' That's how Mom looked at salvation. All her kids needed it…to survive. It was a life-or-death situation for her and her children. And when you think about it, to choose or not choose Jesus really *is* a life-or-death situation for every person. So Mom never backed down."

We all want our daughters to thrive in their spiritual life. But sometimes, we get the idea that once they get to a certain age and start to resist our attempts to nurture them spiritually, that's when we should back off.

We live in a world that tells Christians "Don't push Jesus on people" because it's not politically correct to do so. We hear from others that "Your faith is personal, so you shouldn't talk about it." We also live in a day and age when, sadly, too many people have a poor opinion of the church. So when your preteen or teenage daughter says, "I don't want to go to church anymore," or "I don't want to go to *that* church anymore," or she flat-out tells you, "I don't know if I believe in your God anymore," we tend to wring our hands helplessly and think, *What can I do*?

Lots, my friend. Starting by not backing down.

The Fruit of a Mom's Determination

Listen to the testimonies of daughters who, at one time, might have accused their parents of "pushing Jesus" or "preaching too much" or "pushing the church" on them.

Katie, who is now 29 and has a child of her own, says, "One thing I will always appreciate is that my parents insisted we attend church *every* Sunday. In my rebellious years, I hated it and gave them a bad attitude about it. As an adult, however, I realize it was the greatest gift they could have given me.

"My best memories are youth retreats and summer camps. I did most of my spiritual growth then. I will always remember the Bible verse about training up your child in the way he should go and when he is old, he will not depart from it [see Proverbs 22:6]. I think about that all the time with the child I am now raising. I feel it is my responsibility as a good parent— and it is a conviction in my heart—to give him those same opportunities and experiences I had."

Denise, 49, who raised two children and is now a grandmother, says, "The most important thing that my mom and dad did for me was raise me in a Christian home. That was the most important thing, so I wanted to make sure I did that as well."

And she did. Her daughter, Brooke, a 30-year-old mom of two small children, says, "My mom made going to church a regular thing. I appreciate her discipline in her faith and establishing that discipline in me. I want my children to be exposed to strong biblical teaching and be surrounded by believers each Sunday, if not more often. Even when my dad wouldn't go to church, my mom would still go and take us kids. Her determination was always admirable."

It Comes Down to Mom

Some moms feel inadequate to guide their daughters spiritually. For some it's because they feel they don't know enough of the Bible; for others, it's because they don't feel confident about praying out loud. For still others, it's because they haven't been in a relationship with God long enough to help their daughter know how to function in a relationship with Christ.

But whatever your situation, don't sell yourself short. Remember, because of your constant presence in your daughter's life, she will pick up on your faith if it is genuine. Most daughters attribute their spiritual background to their mothers, regardless of how spiritual (or unspiritual) their mothers were.

A young woman I'm discipling recently told me: "Even though my mom's relationship with God has been all over the place the last few years, she is the one who taught me to pray and to attend church. She is the primary person who introduced me to my beliefs.

"Even though I lived with her only during the first twelve years of my life, I remember seeing my mom reading her Bible and volunteering each year to help with vacation Bible school. I also remember her saying, 'Hold on to Jesus.' She often claimed Jesus as her rock, even though she didn't live it a lot of the time. But that was something I remember hearing."

And it's something that young woman is doing today—holding on to Jesus.

Kelly, now 30, says, "I am thankful that my mom talked to me about

God and Jesus. I am so thankful she church-shopped for years so I could learn how important worship is in my faith journey. I am glad she shared about her negative church experiences yet still believed in God. I do wish, though, I would have seen her pray, read the Bible, and encourage me to learn more about the Christian life."

Don't underestimate the value of laying a spiritual foundation for your daughter. If you have already set that foundation, even if it was basic and long ago, it's never too late to start building on it. And, isn't having a daughter, and knowing that eternity is at stake for her, enough of a reason to *get to know* the Bible well and learn to pray confidently and be the spiritual mentor she will inevitably need?

Guidelines for Shepherding Her Heart

I want to provide some practical guidelines for you when it comes to shepherding your daughter's heart. But at the same time, I don't want to focus on rules in this chapter. Rather, I want to emphasize *relationship*. Providing for you a list of "dos and don'ts" will not draw your daughter's heart toward God or keep it there if she has been raised to know the truth. As was discussed in the last chapter, she will learn more by what she sees in your relationship with God and your relationship with her. It's not just a matter of *what* you believe in, but *Whom* you believe in. It's not just what you claim, but how you live. It's not about the rules you try to enforce, it's all about a relationship with Christ that you can model for her so that she desires the same for her own life. And it's about what you do to keep a loving, respectful relationship with her.

Make It Fun

If your daughter is young, make your faith fun. Make it an adventure. Make it more than about just taking her to church or requiring Bible reading. The Christian life is not an assignment. Nor is it one of our "daily chores." It is a love relationship. And the more enjoyable and exciting your faith is, the more enjoyable and exciting it will be for her.

Rebekah Montgomery (whom I quoted earlier in chapter 7, who came from a long line of influential and inspiring women) says her fervor for the Lord, her heart for prayer, and her compassion for people that spurred her toward evangelism as a way of life didn't develop by chance. Her mother modeled it all in front of her.

"My mom made spirituality fun and natural," Rebekah said. "We had our own Bible club—just Mom and us kids. On club days, we would fly through the housework and put on our club rings (especially made and engraved with IAH—I Am His), and Mom would plan a romp in the woods with a lunch she'd packed. And she would teach us a Bible lesson about something specific.

"Also, since there were eight of us kids and one bathroom, school mornings could be a bit hectic. She put up a big blackboard and wrote one Bible verse on it each day. While we were waiting in line for the bathroom, we were supposed to memorize the verse. She wouldn't let us out the door to get on the bus unless we could say our verse. It made for a lot of laughter and started the day off right."

But in addition to having fun, the family also got real with each other by sharing their hearts with one another.

"We had family devotions at night too. What was shared there was kept inside the family. We knew about mom and dad's financial situation, health, and other concerns because they shared them with us and we all prayed about them. I don't remember being worried about these matters because *they* weren't. There was a sense of excitement and anticipation to see what God would do."

As was the case in Rebekah's family, when your children get older, they will need to see that your faith is not just fun, but real too.

Make It Real

"When I was a child, my mom modeled submission in the home very well," says Brooke. "Mom did all the grunt work that made our family function. She got very little credit in return. She wasn't a martyr, but she really worked hard for the benefit of others; she had a servant's spirit."

But it was seeing her mom handle a crisis that really showed Brooke what her mom was made of. She was a woman who fastened feet to her faith and lived it out in spite of what she was feeling or what life dealt her.

"As an adult, I watched my mom endure a crisis in her marriage. She reflected Christ in her forgiveness and humility. She dropped all her ego and made recovering her marriage a priority. She committed to digging into her relationship with Christ for strength. So, most recently, her dependence on the Lord and focus on that above all relationships has inspired and had an impact on me."

What better way for our daughters to grab hold of our faith than when they see us living it out in the grittiness of life? No one, our daughters included, wants something that we just talk about but don't live. Your daughter is (or will someday be) too busy to want to spend her Sunday mornings in church or take time to be in God's Word regularly or put herself in a place where she can serve God with her life if it isn't something she is convinced is worthwhile. And your greatest testimony to that is what you share with her about how God has come through for you, or what she sees for herself, about how Christ has impacted your life. Our daughters see the reality of our faith, and our struggles and who God is in the midst of them, when we share our heart with them.

Share Your Heart

Pamela, whose mother passed away when she was 27, regrets not having the chance to learn more about what her mom experienced as a young wife and mother.

"I wish I could've heard more as I was growing up—about how my mother felt growing up or how she felt about her personal struggles as a woman, wife, and mother. That would've been helpful as I make my way to better understanding what it means to be a woman, a wife, and a mom. Of course, my mother passed away when I was 27 and just a young mother myself, so I am sure there are discussions that, if I could have them with her now, they would give me that glimpse into the treasury of her heart that I so wish I could glean from today."

Pamela makes an effort to be very real with her own daughter by sharing with her not only her thoughts and feelings, but humbly admitting when she's wrong as well.

"I go to my daughter if I know or feel I have hurt her in some way and I will apologize to her," Pamela said. "I feel it's important for us as parents to be humble and to repent when we have wronged our children. We have to model humility and repentance as well as what forgiveness looks like."

Annemarie, 21, says her mom felt it was a weakness to share so much of her heart and emotions with her daughter, but Annemarie saw it as a strength.

"Although my mom feels ashamed when she is open emotionally—she was taught 'Never air your dirty laundry in public' and 'Avoid conflict at all costs'—it made it so much easier for me to relate to her. It meant that I could trust her, since she could feel the same way I did, and it meant that I could approach her. As I've gotten older, that only rings more true. My mom is like the better me. She and I think similarly, act and react similarly, and experience emotions similarly. I'm able to turn to someone who knows how it feels and has survived.

"So many times my mom and I have clashed and had conflicts—but every time I know she is genuinely trying to figure things out. If we're frustrated with each other, at least we're still willing to talk it out or try to understand the other's point of view. My mom's honesty and authenticity have taught me so much more about how to be a woman than she knows."

Trust Her Heart

In the last chapter we looked at how lack of trust can lead to a battle if your daughter has earned your trust but you're not giving it to her. Trusting her is also essential in guiding her spiritually, because it means you are trusting that God has done a work in her and will continue that work. Our daughters sometimes see our lack of trust in them as a lack of trust in their relationship with God, and that can be hurtful to them.

Cheryl had to trust that God was working in the heart of her teenage foster child whom she adopted. There were days when it didn't look like any spiritual progress was being made. But Cheryl was able to see her own heart and condition before God in that mix and surrender it to God and trust Him with the rest.

"Kaylee and I both have too great a need to be in control," Cheryl said. "The difference is that I know I can, and must, release that need to God. For Kaylee, that is difficult. It is typical for a teenager to reject her parents' beliefs and determine for herself what she believes. My daughter struggles with believing God is all-powerful and loves her when 'He allows such bad things to happen to me.' I need to stop trying to control her spiritual journey and just release her into God's care. If *I* can't trust Him with her heart, how can I expect *her* to trust Him?"

Love Her as God Does

I realize, as I write this, that there are some moms reading this who have done everything in their power to raise their daughters to love and serve God. They have prayed over them and for them. And they have wrestled with God over the choices their daughters have made or where their daughters are today spiritually.

Can I share with you what my youth pastor, Tom, told me shortly after I gave birth to Dana? He said, "God was the perfect parent, but Adam and Eve still sinned." Now I am by no means the perfect parent, nor are you. But just knowing that God did *everything* right—in terms of parental love, expectations, outlining the rules, providing opportunities, and granting freedom—and Adam and Eve *still* sinned, gives me hope. It reminds me that, unlike Adam and Eve, who had a perfect nature when they were created, our children are sinners, by nature, and they *will* make wrong and foolish choices. They *will* rebel at times. They *will* break our hearts... even if we did most everything right. So rather than beat yourself up for what more you could've done, relate to the heart of your Father God, who knows what it feels like to be disappointed by His children yet loves and forgives them through every disappointment and every act of rebellion.

One mom told me, "I was heartbroken when my daughter chose to not wait until marriage to have an intimate relationship with the man who is now her husband. I felt like I had done something wrong in preparing her for life in that aspect, even though we talked about so many things, even the possibility of an unplanned pregnancy. But I was still completely heartbroken. I felt like such a failure. Then I realized that I was human and that no matter what, God still loved my daughter, and He still loved me."

In 1 Corinthians 13:7, God's Word says true biblical love "bears all things, believes all things, hopes all things, endures all things" (NASB). In another Bible translation, that verse says:

> [Love] puts up with anything,
> Trusts God always,

Always looks for the best,
Never looks back,
But keeps going to the end (MSG).

Those words can soothe over the bitterness that might start to develop in our hearts if our daughters have disappointed us. Or if they've outright rebelled against us. Maybe by now your daughter has broken your heart in numerous ways. Maybe, at this moment, the thought of her gives you a lump in your throat or a knot in your stomach. We all have our moments like that. But I'm so relieved that our loving heavenly Father *never* gets to the point with us where He says, "Enough! I've had it! Go be someone *else's* problem." God never looks down, shakes His head, and says, "There's no hope. I might as well give up." Instead, God "never looks back, but keeps going to the end" when it comes to His love for us.

When I wrote my book *When a Woman Inspires Her Husband,* I considered, in detail, God's love for me, and it greatly influenced how I began to see—and express love toward—my husband. I realized if I practiced love toward him the way God loves me, our marriage would be different. And my, how our marriage has changed for the better since I started focusing on loving him the way God loves me!

As moms, you and I can apply that same kind of godly love to our daughters and see it completely revolutionize our relationship with them. Look with me at some of the ways God loves us, and let's see how we can love our daughters the same way. I can think of no clearer picture we can give our daughters of Jesus than to be Jesus to them.

Look at the ways God loves us and ask yourself if you are loving your daughter this way, regardless of her age, regardless of where she is, regardless of what she's done, regardless of how she may or may not feel toward you.

He has promised He will never leave you.

Never will I leave you; never will I forsake you (Hebrews 13:5).

Can you say this to your daughter—that you will never leave her emotionally—and truly mean it as God means it toward you?

He is always thinking only the best about you.

> How precious to me are your thoughts, O God! How vast is
> the sum of them! Were I to count them, they would outnum-
> ber the grains of sand (Psalm 139:17-18).

Can you say that you only think—and say—the best about your
daughter? Even if other moms all around you are complaining about their
children?

He is gentle toward you when you're broken.

> He heals the brokenhearted, and binds up their wounds
> (Psalm 147:3).

God never says, "Serves you right," or "I told you so." Are you gentle
toward your daughter even when she is angry or unlovable—which is how
people sometimes respond when they're hurt?

He promises nothing will ever come between the two of you.

> [Nothing] will be able to separate us from the love of God
> (Romans 8:39).

Are there any conditions or exceptions in your mind when it comes to
loving your daughter? Is there something in the back of your mind that
she could do that would make you turn your back on her and disown her
as a daughter? God holds no such reservations about you. He has promised that *nothing*—and that includes anything you might do—will ever
come between the two of you. That is persevering love. Do you have that
kind of love toward your daughter?

He delights in you, quiets you with His love, and sings over you.

> He will rejoice over you with gladness, He will quiet you with
> His love, He will rejoice over you with singing (Zephaniah
> 3:17 NKJV).

Can you delight in your daughter and rejoice over her simply because of who she is—one who is loved by her heavenly Father and by you?

He loved you so much He was willing to die so He wouldn't have to live without you.

> God so loved the world that he gave his one and only Son, that whoever believes in him shall not perish but have eternal life (John 3:16).

God gave up what meant the most to Him so He wouldn't have to be separated from you for eternity. Are you willing to do what it takes so your daughter can know what it means to trust God with her soul and live eternally with Him?

He loved you in spite of yourself and still does.

> God demonstrates his own love for us in this: While we were still sinners, Christ died for us (Romans 5:8).

Would you show sacrificial love to your daughter even if she didn't deserve it? Even if she had turned her back on you?

Scripture tells us:

> This is the kind of love we are talking about—not that we once upon a time loved God, but that he loved us and sent his Son as a sacrifice to clear away our sins and the damage they've done to our relationship with God. My dear, dear friends, if God loved us like this, we certainly ought to love each other.[16]

Now, from what you've seen about God's persevering love for you, you are called to love your daughter...
even when she disappoints you,
even when she's inconsiderate,
even when she's unlovable,
even when she's clearly wrong and unrepentant,
even when she's acting unbearably.

Do you realize, dear mom, that your condemnation will push her away, whereas your love will soften her heart and wear her down? Mostly it will model before her God's love for her. Again, God never says, "I'm so tired of this; she's not worth it." God patiently waits for *your* heart. You patiently wait for *hers*.

When She's Resistant

I know that as I write this there will be readers who feel it is too late to guide their daughters spiritually. Maybe your daughter seems too far gone at this point, or too far into rebellion, or too wrapped up in a life without God, that you can't see her ever turning around and coming back home to a faith in and thriving personal walk with God.

Whether your daughter is in rebellion right now or just fails to meet your expectations for her, 1 Corinthians 13:7 gives you godly wisdom on how to deal with it. There, we are reminded that godly love "bears all things, believes all things, hopes all things, endures all things" (NASB).

In chapter 2, I shared this passage so we could see what kind of love God has for us. But now I want us to look at it as the kind of love a mother can show toward her daughter if it looks like, from a spiritual standpoint, she is a long way from home.

If that is true about your daughter, you need to keep *bearing* with her, *believing* in her, *hoping* she will come around, and *enduring* with her. That is godly love. To love your daughter in these ways means loving her regardless of her actions. You can love her without excusing or condoning her behavior. You can love her even if she is breaking your heart—and God's. You can love her in spite of her actions and choices.

You can love her because God first loved you (1 John 4:19).

A Mom's Choice to Love

Linda" is a woman who has chosen to love her daughter with open arms rather than cross her arms and insist her daughter meet her (and God's) expectations before returning home.

Listen to this wise woman who is choosing to love her daughter with a 1 Corinthians 13:7 kind of love that "bears all things, believes all things, hopes all things, endures all things"—regardless of her daughter's choices and lifestyle.

"My daughter was an outstanding student and student government leader, and captain of the basketball team at her Christian high school. I didn't come to know the Lord until she was 13, and then I sent her and her brother to a Christian school after her sister ended up a runaway at 16 and her dad and I split over his drug use and girlfriend. Prior to that, we were a 'perfect-looking family.' We ran a medium-size family business, won lots of awards, joined the country club. Our kids were successful actors in Hollywood. For sixteen years my two daughters were in the top 95 percent of Screen Actors Guild earners.

"High school took my girls out of acting because they wanted to participate in sports. 'Jean,' my second child, was a top achiever. She was the best apologist in her class at her Christian high school and was a leader of Senior Girls Bible Study, which met at our home. She went on a church missions trip to Venezuela the summer after her junior year. It was a difficult trip and they had to deal with a death, political unrest, and so on. Her boyfriend broke her heart that year, and her dad had broken her heart when she was 13.

"Off she went to college—a long distance from our home. At five-feet, three-inches tall, she was too small to play regular basketball at college, but played in the pickup games. Her second year, her grades slipped, and she told me she was coming home to buy a house with her acting money because it was too expensive to buy where she had been attending school. I then found out from a friend who visited her at school that she had a girlfriend.

"That put me in counseling for three months. I was tormented that my daughter had fallen and walked away from the Lord. She began to be my persecutor. She would rarely talk to me on the phone and would end calls by hanging up on me after saying things like, 'You think I'm going to hell.' I was not preaching to her, but I did ask her what had happened such that she would choose this particular lifestyle. She refused to answer that question. She moved closer to home with that girlfriend and bought a house at 20 years old. She was working successfully, as always. She has a strong entrepreneurial spirit.

"When I saw my daughter and her friend, I tried to show love to them both, and the Lord allowed me to see their brokenness. That girlfriend broke her heart. The next girlfriend stayed with her for a couple of years, and they were politically active. Every time we spoke, my daughter would throw some angry bomb at me. I had decided, through God's prompting, not to respond anymore to the attacks. Instead, I would counter each one with, 'But I love you.' Or, 'Okay, but I love you.' For a few months the infrequent phone calls continued, but I would not engage in any negative discussion, and I always resorted to the response, 'But I love you.' Eventually we could start talking about what was happening with her dog, how those who were renting rooms in her house were doing, and other matters.

"Jean came to see me here at our ranch at Christmas, and we had a wonderful time being mother and daughter. I kissed her temples, and she let me. We laughed and didn't have to talk about politics. She is not with a girlfriend now and calls me every week or so. We had spoken frankly about her stand, and she said it was a relief to tell me some of the things she had encountered on her life road. I do not ask details, but I can listen. It is loving. She even told me that finding a dog walker in her neighborhood was what I would call 'a godsend.' I agreed. My stand is that Jesus will never forget her or let her go, so I can release her into His hands and trust Him with her heart. My job is to show His love toward her until the day she embraces Him once again."

. . . .

Jesus told a story about this kind of love in Luke 15:11-31. The youngest of two sons asked his father for his share of his inheritance. Now, there could have been quite a battle when that son asked for his inheritance early. In Jewish culture, to do that was the equivalent of saying, "I wish you were dead. So give me *now* what you owe me."

Though that was not an acceptable request, the father gave him the money anyway. This young man then left home, went off to a foreign country, and foolishly squandered all the money on drinking binges and prostitutes.

Without a cent to his name, he ended up hiring himself out to a foreigner, feeding pigs. So destitute was he that he longed to eat at least what the pigs were eating so he wouldn't starve. Eventually he realized he'd be better off returning home and facing scorn and punishment for his actions, and living out the rest of his days as one of his father's hired men. At least that would mean he wouldn't starve.

So, with head hung low in shame, he returned home. His father, according to Jewish custom, should have kept his dignity and reputation in the community by considering his son dead and never acknowledging him again. Yet, this father never lost hope for his son. Evidently he was watching the road, maybe even daily, for his son to return. Scripture tells us that while the son was "still a long way off," his father saw him and was filled with compassion for him" (verse 20).

What the father did next—before his son even had a chance to apologize—is shocking. With no regard for his personal dignity, he hiked up his robe and *ran* to meet his son. *Raced* for him. Full-on beat it down the path so he could throw his arms around his son and cry and hug and kiss his dirty, foul-smelling body (which had traveled a long distance and probably slept in a pig stall!). Then the father killed his best calf, roasted it, and threw a party in celebration of his son's return home.

The emphasis in Jesus' story was not on the young man's rebellion, nor on his repentance, but on the father's compassion and unreserved forgiveness. Jesus told the story so we, as children of God and as parents of children, would understand the unfailing, persevering, forgiving love of our heavenly Father.

This story offers a beautiful picture of how we can love our own children when they choose to live differently than we had hoped. When they break our hearts. When they rebel against our authority. When they turn their backs on our values and beliefs and demand that we owe them something. When they take everything we've given them and decide to live ungratefully for themselves.

This story models for us the forgiving heart of a parent. Love "bears all things, believes all things, hopes all things, endures all things." That kind of love, according to 1 Corinthians 13:8, "never fails."

Keep On Believing

Today, Linda holds on to hope that her daughter will one day return to the arms of her Savior. And this mother takes comfort in knowing her heavenly Father desires Jean's return even more than she does.

God holds your daughter's heart in His hands. Trust Him with it. And show her the love your Father has shown you. Like the forgiving father of the prodigal son, Linda is watching the road, waiting for her daughter to come home when she finds that this world and what it offers will not satisfy. And when Jean does come home, her mother's arms will be wide open to welcome her.

Shepherding Your Daughter's Heart ······························

1. Insert your daughter's name on the lines below, and then picture her face, her heart, her recent actions. As you read this passage, let these words pour over your heart for her:

> Love [for (insert your daughter's name here)] is patient and kind. Love [for _____] is not jealous or boastful or proud or rude. It does not demand its own way. It is not irritable, and it keeps no record of being wronged. It does not rejoice about injustice but rejoices whenever the truth wins out. Love [for _____] never gives up, never loses faith, is always hopeful, and endures through every circumstance (NLT).

2. Read the story of the Prodigal Son in Luke 15:11-31.

a. What impresses you the most about the father's reaction to his rebellious son?

b. To which character can you most relate—the rejected, forgiving father? The rebellious and then repentant youngest son? Or the older, less-forgiving son? Why?

3. Which aspect of God's love on pages 173–75 means the most to you? How can you show that kind of love toward your daughter?

A Prayer for Her Heart

God, You know it is my utmost desire to see my daughter love You and walk in Your ways. Yet I can only do so much. I trust You to give me the wisdom I need to encourage her obedience to You and then to know when I need to just quietly trust You to keep her in Your hands. May I model to her the joy and passion of a love relationship with You so that all her life she desires that as well. And may she and I share a similar mind and heart when it comes to knowing You, loving You, and desiring to serve You. Lord, I entrust her into Your capable hands. And regardless of the decisions she makes, help me to continually *be* the woman I long for her to become spiritually.

Chapter 10

Becoming Her Best Friend

Her children respect and bless her;
her husband joins in with words of praise:
"Many women have done wonderful things,
but you've outclassed them all!"

PROVERBS 31:28-29 MSG

As you've taken this journey with me, my prayer has been that you've already come to see your relationship with your daughter grow and blossom. It is my hope that by now you are well on your way to her seeing you as a loving friend she can trust.

You've probably heard it said as many times as I have that you can't be your daughter's friend; you must be her parent. And that is true...when your daughter is 5. And when she is 10. And especially when she is a teenager. But somewhere between the ages of 18 and 21, when she realizes she has the ability and the right to make decisions on her own, that's when you want to be one of the women she respects most and the one from whom she seeks advice. As she becomes a wife and a mother herself, that's when you want to be the one she calls first when she needs to share her heart. All through her adult life, I'm sure you want her to consider you a close friend, if not her closest friend.

Earning that kind of respect in your daughter's life happens when you've built her up, given her the gift of your time, entered her world, encouraged her to dream, given her wings, chosen your battles well, and mentored her spiritually. When she's an adult, you want her to see you as someone who respects her as much as she respects you—and someone who will still tell her what she needs to hear, not just what she wants to hear.

One day while Dana was in her preteen years, I was venting over the phone with my sister about how Dana would come unglued with me if I asked her if she'd combed her hair that morning or why she was choosing to wear a particular outfit.

"I don't know what her problem is," I told my sister. "Maybe it's the hormones starting to kick in."

My sister, who has raised only boys, still had the wisdom I needed to hear when it came to raising a daughter: "Cindi, as Dana gets older, it may be time for you to start treating her and talking to her as you would a friend."

"But I'm not her friend, I'm her *parent*," I insisted.

"Of course you are," Kristi said. "But if a friend had a bad breakout one morning, would you say to her, 'You really need to do a better job of washing your face before bed each night'?" Kristi explained that Dana was beyond the age of needing instruction and instead, needed encouragement more than critique.

"She gets insulted just as anyone would," Kristi explained. "She gets embarrassed. Ask yourself: Would I say this in the same way if I was saying it to a girlfriend?"

As Kristi talked, I began to realize that certain statements I intended to be helpful for Dana would sound critical, patronizing, and even rude if I said them to a girlfriend. No wonder my daughter was reacting the way she was!

Since that day, I've tried to use the "friend" filter to help me determine what I should say to Dana. It has helped me narrow down my advice to only what is helpful and courteous. And I've found that the principle I began to apply when Dana was 12 or 13 still applies today. I have learned to talk to Dana as a young woman, a friend, a woman whom I respect.

Now that Dana is an adult, I've noticed she is doing the same with *me*. If I am wearing something unstylish (it's amazing how our views about what is stylish differs these days—I like to think I dress more classic than according to the latest fashion), Dana will soften her comment by saying, "I like your dress, Mom, but I think you should try losing the belt. The outfit would look better with a chunky necklace, don't you think?" My heart softens as I realize she is now trying to say, nicely, the things I used to say to her. (And, for the most part, she continues to say it nicely, even when she has to tell me for the *billionth* time not to wear a zebra print watch or carry a zebra-print purse when I'm wearing a zebra print skirt! "Only *one* loud accessory or print, Mom, not several!") My, how the roles reverse when you age. And oh, how we want our daughters to speak as kindly to us, if not kinder, than we once spoke to them.

Making the Transition

It is our job to raise our children to be independent of us and dependent on God. A little girl needs a mom. But a young woman needs a friend. And you and I can become our daughters' close friend by gradually redefining our role in their lives.

"You never stop being a parent, but you do it in a different way," says my friend Janet Thompson. "You can't demand anymore. You can't ground her. But hopefully you will have built up enough respect to still be her parent. Building that respect relationship is about meeting her where she is, being interested in what she's interested in, and learning to ask questions."

Shea, whose story opens chapter 2, says this about transitioning from the difficult mother-daughter stage to the close friendship stage: "My mother made the transition from mother to friend easily. I'm not sure exactly when it happened, but one day my mother became my friend, and she let go. She left major decisions up to me, and trusted that she had done her best. I'm not sure all young women can say this, but my mom is my friend, and it is so great to do life together with her now!"

Annie, at 21, says she and her mom have finally reached the age where they can enjoy each other: "She's still my mother, but we're past the point of her trying to mother me or smother me. We have a lot of the same interests, ideas, values, thoughts, beliefs. It's nice having her on the same page with me, spiritually and academically. It's a safe place for me now, to have so much compatibility with my mom."

Secrets to Being Her Best Friend

Think about the qualities of a best friend—honesty, loyalty, unconditional support, acceptance, transparency, the ability to keep certain things confidential, someone who allows you to be yourself without condemning or critiquing you. Those are qualities you most likely seek out in others. And when you find them all in one person, you have found a best friend. It's those character qualities that *you* want to develop so that you can *be* that best friend for your daughter.

As I mentioned in chapter 5, when I was interviewing mothers and daughters for this book, I noticed that some of the closest mother-daughter relationships were between stepmoms and stepdaughters. As I talked with them more, I discovered each stepmom had been deliberate and intentional in taking an interest in her stepdaughter's world. And I also found two other elements that contributed to the closeness of their relationships:

1. The stepmom had a "*limited time*" situation with her stepdaughter so she had to focus on making each moment together count.

2. The stepmom was aware of *boundaries* in the relationship, so she worked at establishing trust and respecting those boundaries.

As I pondered this, I realized these two elements have been in place in my relationship with my own stepmom too. I've also found that if you and I implement these two elements in our relationship with our daughters, as well as a few other elements, we can draw them closer to our hearts too.

Adopt a "Limited Time" Perspective

Judy today has a close relationship with her stepdaughter, Sherry. And she attributes that to years of having to make every moment count when Sherry came to visit twice a month.

"We had to make our time valuable and meaningful," Judy said. "We were always aware that we had limited time together, so we made an effort to make every moment of the weekend count. My husband and I didn't spend our time complaining about messy rooms and majoring on the minors. Some things you have to let go."

Apparently that "make each moment count" motto drew their hearts together, ensuring that they developed a quality relationship, because Sherry says, "I still love my mom a lot, but my relationship with my stepmom is closer than it is with my own mom."

Chris also focused on what really matters in her relationship with her stepdaughter, Cristina, even after Cristina moved in at the age of 13. She made sure to look at the big picture of developing a relationship with her daughter rather than nitpicking on minor incidents.

I myself finally got this through my head after Dana left for college. Now that she's only home on the weekends, my desire is to make our times together memorable and enjoyable, rather than harp on her about non-essentials. What a precious element was added to our relationship once I was determined to make each moment with her count!

These days, when she's downstairs and I'm upstairs and she calls for something, instead of saying, "Can't you get it yourself?" my response is, "Sure, let me help you with that." I began to enjoy serving her because I don't have the opportunity to do that often anymore. And she began to enjoy being at home a little more. (Now that doesn't mean she no longer helps out when she's home. She still folds laundry and cleans and even offers to cook for us. The more we, as her parents, serve her, the more she develops a heart for serving us and others.)

Respect Her Boundaries

Cristina became Chris's stepdaughter when she was just 5 years old, but didn't start living with her and her father until she was 13. Although she says it was difficult at first, Chris won her heart by earning her trust and treating Cristina respectfully, something she still does to this day.

"We have mutual love and support for each other," Chris says. "I really do respect her."

Cristina says, "My relationship with my mom [she calls Chris her mom] today is very different than it was years ago. I think because we've both grown a lot in the Lord. My mom earned my trust by being consistent. I needed stability, routine, unconditional love, support, and affection back then."

What means the most to Cristina today in her relationship with Chris? "The partnership I have with her," she said, with tears in her eyes. "I feel her complete support, as a friend, in ministry, in any area of need that I have."

As our daughters age, we can start distancing ourselves from them without even realizing it by being critical of them or their decisions, meddling in their affairs, offering advice when it's not asked for, and so on. So we must be aware of our boundaries as moms once our daughters become young women. And one very important boundary is waiting until we are asked before we offer advice or jump in to help them.

Chris said that is something we can do through the help of the Holy Spirit.

"I really credit God for it. In my own self I don't think it would be that easy [to respect Cristina's boundaries]. Sometimes it's hard to keep my mouth shut. I do wear my heart on my sleeve, and I tend to be vocal."

Chris said she runs her words through the filter of Philippians 4:8 (as we talked about in chapter 3) as a guideline for what to say and how to provide input for her adult daughter, who is now married and has a family of her own.

"I do love that passage—whatever is lovely, whatever is praiseworthy, think and speak on those things," Chris said.

"We have transitioned over time. I'm still her mom. I am also her friend. But she's also very good about keeping parts of her life private. I try not to get into her business. I try to come alongside her without meddling. I also want to be respectful of her husband, who was raised differently, and not undermine him.

"If I tear down rather than build up, she's not going to want me to visit or spend time with their daughter. If I tear them down, that burns a bridge."

Several moms who have close friendships with their daughters today offered the following wisdom when it comes to giving advice or expressing your disagreement with something your daughter is doing.

Say It Lovingly

God calls the older woman to train the younger. So you and I can have confidence when it comes to sharing sound, godly wisdom with our daughters—wisdom that we've prayed about and have received the "green light" from God to share it with them.

Chris says, "I use the line, 'I know you haven't asked me about this, but I feel compelled to share this with you.' She and her husband already know that I am passionate about seeing them do well in their lives, both physically and spiritually."

"Or," Chris offers, "I will say, 'Honey, have you ever thought about...?' And she might say, 'Nope, I haven't.' But she can confidently say that. And there are no hurt feelings."

Ask Questions

Janet said she used to struggle with how to approach her daughter when she felt Kim was making decisions that weren't the best for herself or her family. She didn't want to appear critical, nor did she want to offer unsolicited advice. But then God impressed it upon her heart that it's okay to ask questions.

"When your daughter knows how you feel about an issue but then tells you what she's doing and wants your opinion, then that's an indication you can ask her questions."

By asking questions, Janet gives her daughter a chance to think through her decisions and explore every possible angle. Sometimes during the question-and-answer session, her daughter will realize she has other options or there are problems she hadn't considered. At times she will reconsider. But if she decides to stay with her original decision, Janet now has the assurance that her daughter has, in fact, thought the decision through and knows what she's doing and why.

Janet added that it's also important that we as moms be okay with not having to get the credit or recognition when we help our daughters arrive at a better decision: "We have to put pride aside and not have to be right all the time and have them recognize we're right. Who cares how they arrived at their decision as long as they did the right thing?"

Be the Peacemaker

As you and your daughter age, it's possible one—or both—of you will become more stubborn. If that is the case, *you* be the one who takes the initiative to extend grace and keep the peace.

Chris says if there's ever a rift or disagreement between her and her daughter, she believes it's her responsibility, as the mom, to make sure the relationship is running smoothly. "I feel it's more the job of the older woman to make sure she has a relationship with her daughter or stepdaughter or daughter-in-law. Why wouldn't I want to get along with her?

"A lot of times women our age [forties and fifties] are kind of jealous of their daughters because of missed opportunities from the past, but why wouldn't we want our daughters to have an excellent marriage or a great relationship with God?"

Let Her Grow Up

We talked in chapter 7 about preparing your daughter for life and help-ing her develop wings. Sometimes we need to relearn the necessity of let-ting go. There will come times when you want to rush to your daughter's assistance or come on strong in response to a decision you feel isn't in her best interest. But one of the most important gifts you can give your daugh-ter is trusting her to live a sensible, responsible, and God-honoring life. Doing that is an act of friendship.

Tracie, who believed her mom held too tightly to her as she was grow-ing up, says this about their relationship today: "My mom and I have a close adult friendship, and I am grateful for this. What I need most now is my mom's trust in my ability to take care of myself, and also for her to rely on godly women her own age rather than completely upon me for her emotional health. Although I am a forty-two-year-old single woman, my lack of a husband or a family of my own suggests to my mom that she needs to be even more concerned for my well-being; she is concerned that I am alone. Her concern can sometimes be frustrating or even demeaning. I know she doesn't intend to come across this way, but I can't help feeling that she does not believe I can take care of myself.

"It also makes me think that I am incomplete without a spouse or a family of my own. This is not my mom's intent, but it comes across in a subconscious way that impacts me greatly.

"I do not want to complain too strongly about this—I would so much rather have a mother who cares for me a bit too much than one who doesn't! But there is a side-effect…a feeling of being smothered sometimes and a desire to feel more 'in control.'

"My mom and I have talked about this, and she has made huge strides in trying to understand my views and the extent to which her excessive concern makes me feel incomplete and even more alone. I love my mom for trying so hard to let go and let me grow up.

"She is also making an effort to connect with women her age—a circle of friends she can confide in and socialize with. I love doing things with my mom and chatting with her on the phone, but I know God will bless her so much—and even improve our relationship—through her investment in godly friends."

Be Teachable

Did you hear Tracie's heart for her mom? Just as her mom wanted what was best for Tracie all her life, Tracie now wants what's best for her mom. And just as *you* want the best for your daughter, when you both get older, there will be times your daughter expresses her desire for *your* best. She will be able to see some things in your life that need correction, redirection, or more attention from you. Be teachable and open to her observations and advice. What goes around comes around in relationships. Be mature and generous and make sure you respond to your daughter in the same way you want her to respond to you.

Being open to your daughter's advice will help draw you two closer together. It is humbling to hear from our daughters how we can be better examples in our faith or make wiser decisions as we age. By listening and receiving advice from her, you are showing your respect for her, as well as your maturity.

Keep Inspiring Her

Before I close out this chapter I want to share with you the character traits of moms that daughters said they most wanted to imitate. These character qualities were the seeds of inspiration that moms planted in the hearts of their daughters. And those seeds grew into a love and respect and friendship that these daughters want to continue with their moms today. Hopefully you will see many of these qualities in yourself and be reminded of just how important they are to your daughter. View this list of characteristics as a tribute to you—or a checklist for your life:

Your Heart for Others

"My mom's generosity and openheartedness have greatly shaped who I am," says Christen, now 23. "My mom has always had a heart to help others. So when my friends have needed help, I have felt free to ask my mom if we can help them. She comes alongside me in those ventures, and I feel as if my mother's willingness to do this has given me the desire and capability to help others."

Tracie echoes those statements about her mom: "My mom is the consummate caregiver. She has such a selfless, giving, and generous spirit. I aspire to be like her in this way. She has taken care of me in my many times of need—when I was recovering from surgeries, or when I was trying to remodel my kitchen so that I could sell my house. She will drive for hours to help me unpack from a move or to take care of my cat (which she is allergic to), or even fly across an ocean to stay with me for five weeks, which she did while I was going through a difficult time. She also has taken care of my dad when he was gravely ill—at the hospital every day and taking care of intimate physical needs when he was recovering. When her friends are in need, she is there. When strangers are in need, she is there. I admire her so much for this amazing quality...if I could be half as generous and caring as she is, I would be a fortunate woman."

Your Experience as a Mother

You've traveled the road before your daughter. And you've been some places she hasn't. And your experience is valuable to her, perhaps no more than when she becomes a mom herself.

Brooke says, "My mom is my go-to person for most things, but I think I reach out to her the most about my kids. Now that I'm raising kids I have so much more respect for my mom, who basically did the parenting alone while my dad's job kept him away a lot. My brother and I used to pull the same shenanigans that my kids are already trying on me. I place a lot more value on my mom now that I'm a mother."

Your Unwavering Support

Lauren says, "My mom did an awesome job encouraging me and being on my side, even if it seemed like the wrong time in my head. She was quick to give me wise insight in my life. I think it took a little while for us to work out the kinks, but my mom is my best friend. I know she will hear me out and love me no matter what. She loves and accepts me for who I am and doesn't try to change me."

Your Integrity

"The aspect I value most in my relationship with my mom is the mutual respect we have for each other," Christen said. "Over the course of my adult life, I have grown to appreciate the circumstances that have shaped and molded my mother's belief system. I have been able to come to an understanding of my mother's feelings, fears, strengths, weaknesses, and passions. I feel as though she too has been able to see me grow as an individual and a Christian. We enthusiastically appreciate many of the same ideals and beliefs, and respectfully accept the issues on which we differ." Katie, who didn't like that her mom was so insistent upon her spiritual growth and development during her teenage years, says this today about her relationship with her mom: "I absolutely love the relationship that I have with my mom today. I have made some hard choices to be honest with her about things I never wanted her to know, and it made for some uncomfortable days and weeks of disappointment. But, in the end, I am glad I came clean. I don't have to keep secrets anymore, and our relationship now is based on truth. It's raw and funny, and when I need advice, I know she is just a phone call away."

Your Loving Discipline

Christen says, "My mom's view on discipline has greatly impacted who I am." She said rather than having a set punishment for everything, her mother believed in punishments that fit the crime. "Never have I felt that my mom overpunished me as a child or a teenager. I was very sensitive as a young child, and I didn't need a spanking for everything I did wrong. She understood that and took into account my nature, and never squashed it. Many times, the natural consequences of my wrong actions punished me much worse than my mother ever did. The fact that she allowed me to experience these consequences has grown me into a more cautious person who does not allow her impulsivity and fleshly desires to get the better of her. Also, this balanced stance on discipline has kept me from embitterment, which has led me to love and cherish my mother even more, leading to the deepening and strengthening of our relationship."

Chelsea enjoys a close relationship with her parents today as well, and she says one of the reasons is how her parents handled boundaries and disciplinary issues with her: "I was born four months premature and had some life-threatening issues as a newborn, including flat-lining in the delivery room," Chelsea says. "So naturally my parents were very protective of me.

"However," she says, "boundaries and restrictions were never to keep me from doing something bad, but rather to keep something bad from happening to me. I always saw their restrictions as a fence of protection around me, and my parents were careful to let me know that was their intention. Also, my parents never disciplined me out of anger or frustration. Every time I was disciplined, I remember my dad or mom praying with me before and after I received my punishment."

And Shea, who is now a mom herself, said, "It will be important for me to find the balance of love and discipline my mom did. I never once doubted her love for me through her discipline, even though at times I *really* didn't like her for it. As a mom now, I will do my best to be the example my mom was in disciplining me because she loved me and wanted better for me—better decisions, better responsibilities, a better life in general."

Your Sacrifice—on Her Behalf

Don't ever think your daughter won't notice the ways you have sacrificed for her.

Christen said, "My mom laid down her life daily, and continues to do so, in order to raise her children in the ways of the Lord. I want to do that."

Annemarie also admires her mother's selflessness: "The fact that my mom has been there, day in and day out, for my entire life? That's inspiring. She's so selfless. And it's like—she had to be, as a mom. Her life suddenly wasn't hers anymore, and I am in awe of all that she has given of herself."

"Her Courage Under Fire Amazes Me"

After Tracie became an adult, she learned something about her mother that greatly impacted her. "I was so moved by it—and still am. It inspires me to this day," she said.

"My mom got pregnant as a poor, unwed seventeen-year-old in 1969. Soon after giving birth, she was taken to a room—without her mother—and told that she should give me up for adoption. A social worker lectured my mom for nearly two hours about how much better my life would be with a nice, middle-class family and what a selfish person my mom was for refusing to give me up. I can't even imagine how much pressure my mom was under—pressure exerted by people in positions of authority who should have known better. Her courage under fire amazes and inspires me. She could have succumbed to that pressure and given me up for adoption—for a 'better life.' And maybe I would have had a more comfortable life, but I am eternally grateful for my mom's courage and commitment to keeping and raising me. Thinking about how she stood up for me, even when I was an infant, reaffirms for me just how deeply she loves me."

I know you were passionate about your child too when she was born. But if somewhere along the way you lost that spark because of life's circumstances or your daughter's choices or personality differences or time has drawn the two of you apart, you have read this book for a reason. You have put yourself in the place to be taught, encouraged, and equipped. Now be the woman you want your daughter to be. Encourage her the way you wish you were encouraged. Love her like there is no tomorrow—because yours and mine isn't guaranteed.

Their Gift to Us

Our daughters may not become exactly what we've envisioned of them. But then we probably didn't meet our own mother's expectations in every way either. That is where the beauty of our diversity comes into play. That is where we realize our daughter was never our own. She was a gift to us—on loan from God—to shape, influence, mold, and love into a woman who will go on to shape, influence, mold, and love others. The amazing thing is that, as I look back on the first 20 years of my daughter's life, she in many ways shaped and molded *me*. I am much less selfish today now that I've had a daughter to have to sacrifice for, to put first in many ways, and to humbly apologize to on the days when I have messed up. God knew what He was doing in giving me a daughter to influence. He was also placing a woman into my life who would influence *me*.

Dianna can relate. She too was given a gift that she now realizes was God's plan to mold and shape *her* life, as much as she was on assignment to shape her daughter's life.

············· From a Mom's Perspective ·····················

"She's the One Who Inspires Me"

Dianna and her husband, Tracy, had wanted a child for seven years. After multiple miscarriages, they had nearly given up on having a child of their own. But shortly after he returned from the Persian Gulf War in 1991 and they had bought a home, Dianna discovered she had become pregnant.

"I was thrilled and so was Tracy, but we tried to not get too excited due to our past history of miscarriages. I was assigned to a group of high-risk specialists, and our church family began to pray for us. The weeks turned into months, and soon we knew we were having a daughter."

As the months progressed, Dianna's pregnancy became more high risk, and the possibility of her not surviving the pregnancy and childbirth became a real possibility.

"My husband and I spent a lot of time in prayer and discussion. I was at peace for the first time in my entire life because I knew that God was in control."

Little Laura was born six weeks early, and both she and her mother were fine. However, upon arriving home from the hospital, both Tracy and Dianna knew their daughter had some serious issues. She did not seem able to hear.

"After arguing with the Navy Pediatrics Department, I was able to take Laura to see a private pediatrician, who immediately sent us to a hospital, where we discovered that she had a severe hearing loss. Our church family began to pray, my parents began to pray, and we prayed. Laura had surgery, and with speech, occupational, and physical therapy (and much prayer), she overcame her hearing loss.

"The first lesson I taught her as an infant was to give to others. I had a 'meals on wheels' route and I took her along with me. The homebound, elderly, senior adults enjoyed seeing her twice a week more than they did the hot meal. Today, Laura is the most affectionate individual I have ever known, and I firmly believe it is due to her early interaction with those loving souls and their strong prayers.

"Laura has always been a blessing to us and a blessing to anyone who comes into contact with her. She has a gentle spirit, is always full of love, and accepts everyone for whom they are. She accepted Jesus in her heart when she was eight years old because she wanted Him to live within her and guide her through her life.

"Laura has been an inspiration to many people as to what one can accomplish in life. When she was eighteen months old, I was told she would never walk, talk, or accomplish much in her life. Although she has had her own struggles in life, she has overcome each and every one of them. She walks, talks (without ceasing), she is intelligent, witty, and truly loves the Lord. She graduated from high school in 2010 and received her certification as a CNA from the American Red Cross and plans to be a nurse when she finishes college.

"She has volunteered with me in various capacities from working with children and adults with developmental disabilities to encouraging her high school student government adviser to sponsor a day at Panama City Beach for the students of an Alabama high school whose lives were affected by a hurricane.

"I always taught her to think about others before she thought about herself."

Today Laura is married, has a baby of her own, and is still practicing the lessons that her mother taught her about serving others.

"I have tried to inspire my daughter to live a godly life, and she, in turn, has inspired me to do the same. I have had many life-threatening illnesses in my life since Laura's birth, and she has always given me the inspiration to fight and to get better. I always keep one eye on God's Son and one eye on my inspiration, Laura."

Trust the Process

Can you see today how God has molded *you* by giving you the task of molding a daughter? Can you relate to His Father heart for you in your mother heart for your daughter? Do you realize that as much as she means to you, she means even more to God? And as much as you love her, God loves you even more? It is only by God's grace that you can have a positive influence on your daughter and inspire her to lead a godly, influential life. It is only by His help that you can continue to inspire her in the way that you have.

As we complete this journey together, I must ask you: What is your ultimate goal for your daughter? Is it the same as God's—that she live a life worthy of the Lord and please Him in every way, bearing fruit in every good work, growing in the knowledge of God, and being strengthened with all power according to His glorious might so that she will have great endurance, patience, and joy (see Colossians 1:10)? And do you have the same goal for yourself?

Then trust God to have His way in her life—and yours. But realize that, just like you, there will be times when it doesn't show. There will be times when you wonder if you're doing enough. There may be times when it seems she isn't listening. Trust God's work within her heart. And trust the process that God is using to mold your daughter—and you—into the women He wants you both to be.

Drawing Her Heart Toward Yours ·····································

1. Take this opportunity to write a letter to your daughter, telling her of the ways she has inspired you thus far. By encouraging her in this way, you are showing her the incredible potential she has to influence you and others. It is a loving way to build her up and show her that she has become—or soon will be—your best friend.

2. Download my free article entitled "Suggestions for Mother-Daughter Memory Making" on the "Resources and Encouragement" page or the *When a Mom Inspires Her Daughter* book page on my Website at www.StrengthForTheSoul.com. After reading through the article, commit yourself to incorporating a few of the suggestions or coming up with some of your own.

A Prayer of Thanks for This Privilege

God, where do I begin in giving You thanks for this wonderful privilege You have given me to help shape, influence, and inspire not only another person, but a young woman who will, in turn, impact so many others? May I hold each day that we have together—or apart—as another precious opportunity You've given me to inspire her in ways that draw her closer to Your heart and mine. Bless her life—and the lives that she touches—for Your glory. And may You be pleased with how she and I live for the rest of our days.

Closing Words of Encouragement

Thank you for sharing with me this journey to your daughter's heart. I know your time invested in her—and in becoming the woman and mother God wants you to be—will not be wasted. My heart goes with you as you continue to love, support, and inspire your daughter in the days to come.

I would love to hear from you and how you fared on this journey. I would also love to hear the memories you have made or the insights you arrived at as you worked through this book.

Please visit me at www.StrengthForTheSoul.com and let me know how I can pray for you and your daughter(s). My heart remains with you every step of the way.

In His Loving Grip,

Cindi

Appendix

Scriptural Encouragement for Your Daughter

Here are some passages of Scripture you can pray over your daughter. They are arranged by topic so you can find them easily and encourage her when she needs these words most. Write them on a card for her, text them to her when she needs them, or call her at the appropriate time and read them to her. Take the opportunity—as often as you can—to put God's Word into her life—all through her life.

When She is Hurting, Physically or Emotionally

"You intended to harm me, but God intended it for good to accomplish what is now being done" (Genesis 50:20).

"We know that in all things God works for the good of those who love him, who have been called according to his purpose. For those God foreknew he also predestined to be conformed to the image of his Son" (Romans 8:28-29).

"Praise be to the God and Father of our Lord Jesus Christ, the Father of compassion and the God of all comfort, who comforts us in all our troubles, so that we can comfort those in any trouble with the comfort we ourselves receive from God" (2 Corinthians 1:3-4).

"Consider it pure joy, my brothers and sisters, whenever you face trials of many kinds, because you know that the testing of your faith produces perseverance. Let perseverance finish its work so

that you may be mature and complete, not lacking anything"
(James 1:2-4).

When She's Worried About God's Provision

"The lions may grow weak and hungry, but those who seek the
Lord lack no good thing" (Psalm 34:10).

"For the Lord God is a sun and shield;
    the Lord bestows favor and honor;
no good thing does he withhold
    from those whose walk is blameless" (Psalm 84:11).

"The Lord upholds all who fall
    and lifts up all who are bowed down.
The eyes of all look to you,
    and you give them their food at the proper time.
You open your hand
    and satisfy the desires of every living thing" (Psalm 145:14-16).

"My God will meet all your needs according to the riches of his
glory in Christ Jesus" (Philippians 4:19).

When She Needs Confidence in God's Plans for Her

"'My thoughts are not your thoughts neither are your ways my
ways,' declares the Lord. 'As the heavens are higher than the
earth, so are my ways higher than your ways, and my thoughts
than your thoughts'" (Isaiah 55:8-9).

"Our light and momentary troubles are achieving for us an eternal glory that far outweighs them all. So we fix our eyes not on
what is seen, but on what is unseen, since what is seen is tempo-
rary, but what is unseen is eternal" (2 Corinthians 4:17-18).

"Take delight in the Lord,
    and he will give you the desires of your heart.
Commit your way to the Lord;
    trust in him and he will do this" (Psalm 37:4-5).

"I know the plans I have for you," declares the LORD, "plans to prosper you and not to harm you, plans to give you hope and a future" (Jeremiah 29:11).

"We are God's handiwork, created in Christ Jesus to do good works, which God prepared in advance for us to do" (Ephesians 2:10).

When She Feels Insignificant

"You have taken account of my wanderings;
Put my tears in Your bottle.
Are they not in Your book?" (Psalm 56:8 NASB).

"You created my inmost being;
  you knit me together in my mother's womb.
I praise you because I am fearfully and wonderfully made;
  your works are wonderful,
  I know that full well.
My frame was not hidden from you
  when I was made in the secret place,
  when I was woven together in the depths of the earth.
Your eyes saw my unformed body;
  all the days ordained for me were written in your book
  before one of them came to be.
How precious to me are your thoughts, God!
  How vast is the sum of them!
Were I to count them,
  they would outnumber the grains of sand—
  when I awake, I am still with you" (Psalm 139:13-18).

"Can a mother forget the baby at her breast
  and have no compassion on the child she has borne?
Though she may forget,
  I will not forget you!
See, I have engraved you on the palms of my hands;
  your walls are ever before me" (Isaiah 49:15-16).

"Are not two sparrows sold for a penny? Yet not one of them will fall to the ground outside your Father's care. And even the very hairs of your head are all numbered. So don't be afraid; you are worth more than many sparrows" (Matthew 10:29-31).

When She Needs Spiritual Strength or Courage

"We use God's mighty weapons, not worldly weapons, to knock down the strongholds of human reasoning and to destroy false arguments. We destroy every proud obstacle that keeps people from knowing God. We capture their rebellious thoughts and teach them to obey Christ" (2 Corinthians 10:4-5 NLT).

"Now to him who is able to do immeasurably more than all we ask or imagine, according to his power that is at work within us" (Ephesians 3:20).

"Finally, be strong in the Lord and in his mighty power. Put on the full armor of God, so that you can take your stand against the devil's schemes. For our struggle is not against flesh and blood, but against the rulers, against the authorities, against the powers of this dark world and against the spiritual forces of evil in the heavenly realms. Therefore put on the full armor of God, so that when the day of evil comes, you may be able to stand your ground, and after you have done everything, to stand. Stand firm then, with the belt of truth buckled around your waist, with the breastplate of righteousness in place, and with your feet fitted with the readiness that comes from the gospel of peace. In addition to all this, take up the shield of faith, with which you can extinguish all the flaming arrows of the evil one. Take the helmet of salvation and the sword of the Spirit, which is the word of God.

"And pray in the Spirit on all occasions with all kinds of prayers and requests. With this in mind, be alert and always keep on praying for all the Lord's people" (Ephesians 6:10-18).

"Do not be anxious about anything, but in every situation, by prayer and petition, with thanksgiving, present your requests to God. And the peace of God, which transcends all understanding, will guard your hearts and your minds in Christ Jesus" (Philippians 4:6-7).

"Fix your thoughts on what is true, and honorable, and right, and pure, and lovely, and admirable. Think about things that are excellent and worthy of praise" (Philippians 4:8 NLT).

"I can do all things through him who gives me strength" (Philippians 4:13).

When She Is Fearful

"In peace I will lie down and sleep,
    for you alone, LORD,
    make me dwell in safety" (Psalm 4:8).

"His anger lasts only a moment,
    but his favor lasts a lifetime;
weeping may stay for the night,
    but rejoicing comes in the morning" (Psalm 30:5).

"You are my hiding place;
    you will protect me from trouble
    and surround me with songs of deliverance" (Psalm 32:7).

"I waited patiently for the LORD;
    he turned to me and heard my cry.
He lifted me out of the slimy pit,
    out of the mud and mire;
he set my feet on a rock
    and gave me a firm place to stand.
He put a new song in my mouth,
    a hymn of praise to our God.
Many will see and fear the LORD
    and put their trust in him" (Psalm 40:1-3).

"God is our refuge and strength,
    an ever-present help in trouble.
Therefore we will not fear, though the earth give way
    and the mountains fall into the heart of the sea,
though its waters roar and foam
    and the mountains quake with their surging" (Psalm 46:1-3).

"Trust in him at all times, you people;
    pour out your hearts to him,
    for God is our refuge" (Psalm 62:8).

"My help comes from the LORD,
    the Maker of heaven and earth.
He will not let your foot slip—
    he who watches over you will not slumber" (Psalm 121:2-3).

"Where can I go from your Spirit?
    Where can I flee from your presence?
If I go up to the heavens, you are there;
    if I make my bed in the depths, you are there.
If I rise on the wings of the dawn,
    if I settle on the far side of the sea,
even there your hand will guide me,
    your right hand will hold me fast.
If I say, 'Surely the darkness will hide me
    and the light become night around me,'
even the darkness will not be dark to you;
    the night will shine like the day,
    for darkness is as light to you" (Psalm 139:7-12).

"The LORD is gracious and compassionate,
    slow to anger and rich in love.
The LORD is good to all;
    he has compassion on all he has made" (Psalm 145:8-9).

"When you pass through the waters,
    I will be with you;

and when you pass through the rivers,
   they will not sweep over you.
When you walk through the fire,
   you will not be burned;
   the flames will not set you ablaze" (Isaiah 43:2).

"I am convinced that nothing can ever separate us from God's love. Neither death nor life, neither angels nor demons, neither our fears for today nor our worries about tomorrow—not even the powers of hell can separate us from God's love. No power in the sky above or in the earth below—indeed, nothing in all creation will ever be able to separate us from the love of God that is revealed in Christ Jesus our Lord" (Romans 8:38-39 NLT).

When She Feels Lonely or Heartbroken

"By day the LORD directs his love,
   at night his song is with me—
   a prayer to the God of my life" (Psalm 42:8).

"God makes a home for the lonely;
He leads out the prisoners into prosperity,
Only the rebellious dwell in a parched land" (Psalm 68:6 NASB).

"Your decrees are the theme of my song
   wherever I lodge" (Psalm 119:54).

"He heals the brokenhearted
   and binds up their wounds" (Psalm 147:3).

"Your Maker is your husband—
   the LORD Almighty is his name—
the Holy One of Israel is your Redeemer;
   he is called the God of all the earth" (Isaiah 54:5).

"The LORD appeared to us in the past,saying:
'I have loved you with an everlasting love;
   I have drawn you with unfailing kindness'" (Jeremiah 31:3).

"God has said, 'Never will I leave you; never will I forsake you'" (Hebrews 13:5).

When Someone Close to Her Dies

"Even though I walk through the valley of the shadow of death,
    I will fear no evil,
for you are with me;
    your rod and your staff,
    they comfort me" (Psalm 23:4 esv).

"Precious in the sight of the Lord
    is the death of his faithful servants" (Psalm 116:15).

"The Lord cares deeply
    when his loved ones die" (Psalm 116:15 nlt).

"Jesus said to her, 'I am the resurrection and the life. The one who believes in me will live, even though they die; and whoever lives by believing in me will never die. Do you believe this?'" (John 11:25-26).

"If I go and prepare a place for you, I will come back and take you to be with me that you also may be where I am" (John 14:3).

When She Needs Healing

"Surely he took up our pain
    and bore our suffering,
yet we considered him punished by God,
    stricken by him, and afflicted.
But he was pierced for our transgressions,
    he was crushed for our iniquities;
the punishment that brought us peace was on him,
    and by his wounds we are healed" (Isaiah 53:4-5).

"The Spirit of the Lord is upon Me,
Because He has anointed Me

To preach the gospel to the poor.
He has sent Me to heal the brokenhearted,
To proclaim liberty to the captives
And recovery of sight to the blind,
To set at liberty those who are oppressed" (Luke 4:18 NKJV).

When She Feels Guilty or Ashamed

"Then I acknowledged my sin to you
    and did not cover up my iniquity.
I said, 'I will confess
    my transgressions to the LORD.'
And you forgave
    the guilt of my sin" (Psalm 32:5).

"Have mercy on me, O God,
    according to your unfailing love;
according to your great compassion
    blot out my transgressions.
Wash away all my iniquity
    and cleanse me from my sin" (Psalm 51:1-2).

"As far as the east is from the west,
    so far has he removed our transgressions from us" (Psalm
        103:12).

"Search me, God, and know my heart;
    test me and know my anxious thoughts.
See if there is any offensive way in me,
    and lead me in the way everlasting" (Psalm 139:23-24).

"I, even I, am he who blots out
    your transgressions, for my own sake,
    and remembers your sins no more" (Isaiah 43:25).

"I will forgive their wickedness, and will remember their sins no
more" (Jeremiah 31:34).

"You will again have compassion on us;
    you will tread our sins underfoot
    and hurl all our iniquities into the depths of the sea" (Micah
      7:19).

"If we confess our sins, he is faithful and just and will forgive us
our sins and purify us from all unrighteousness" (1 John 1:9).

When She Wants a Fresh Start

"Create in me a pure heart, O God,
    and renew a steadfast spirit within me.
Do not cast me from your presence
    or take your Holy Spirit from me.
Restore to me the joy of your salvation
    and grant me a willing spirit, to sustain me" (Psalm 51:10-12).

"I will give you a new heart and put a new spirit in you; I will
remove from you your heart of stone and give you a heart of flesh"
(Ezekiel 36:26).

"Anyone who belongs to Christ has become a new person. The
old life is gone; a new life has begun!" (2 Corinthians 5:17 NLT).

"I have been crucified with Christ and I no longer live, but Christ
lives in me. The life I now live in the body, I live by faith in the
Son of God, who loved me and gave himself for me" (Galatians
2:20).

Other Harvest House Books
by Cindi McMenamin

When Women Walk Alone

Every woman—whether she's single or married—has walked through the desert of loneliness. Whether you feel alone from being single, facing challenging life situations, or from being the spiritual head of your household, discover practical steps to finding support, transforming loneliness into spiritual growth, and turning your alone times into life-changing encounters with God.

Letting God Meet Your Emotional Needs

Do you long to have your emotional needs met, yet find that your husband or those close to you cannot always help bring fulfillment to your life? Discover true intimacy with God in this book that shows how to draw closer to the lover of your soul and find that He can, indeed, meet your deepest emotional needs.

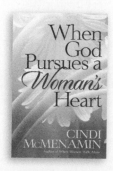

When God Pursues a Woman's Heart

Within the heart of every woman is the desire to be cherished and loved. Recapture the romance of a relationship with God as you discover the many ways God loves you and pursues your heart as your hero, provider, comforter, friend, valiant knight, loving Daddy, perfect prince, and more.

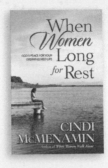

When Women Long for Rest

Women today are tired of feeling overwhelmed by all the demands on their lives and are longing for rest. They want to do more than just simplify or reorganize their lives. *When Women Long for Rest* is an invitation for women to find their quiet place at God's feet—a place where they can listen to Him, open their hearts to Him, and experience true rest.

When a Woman Discovers Her Dream

When it comes to living out the dream God has placed on your heart, do you shrug your shoulders and say, "It's too late…it's too far out of reach…it's too impossible for someone like me"? But you *can* live out that dream—no matter what your stage or place in life. Join Cindi as she shares how you can explore God's purposes for your life, make greater use of your special gifts, turn your dreams into reality, and become the masterpiece God designed you to be.

When a Woman Inspires Her Husband

How can you become your husband's number one fan? God brought you alongside him in marriage to love and support him as only a wife can. Discover how you can be the encourager, motivator, inspiration, and admiration behind your husband—and the wind beneath his wings—as you understand his world, become his cheerleader, appreciate his differences, ease his burdens, and encourage him to dream.

When a Woman Overcomes Life's Hurts

Only God can take the bitter things and turn them into blessings. But healing cannot take place until you uproot the faulty thinking that often accompanies life's wounds and replace it with the truth about how God views you. You'll find this book filled with grace, redemption, and transformation that lead you toward a renewed focus on God, a resurgence of inner joy, and better relationships with others.

When You're Running on Empty

Are you feeling run down and ready to give up? If so, then you're probably running on empty. And you may feel as if the pressures and stress will never end. But there is a way out. Cindi shares from her own life and struggles many helpful and practical secrets about simplifying your priorities and obligations, rejuvenating yourself through God's Word, cultivating health habits that renew your energy, and learning to please God and not people.

Women on the Edge

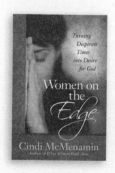

We all have times when we find ourselves on the verge of frustration, despair, or even a meltdown. And we find ourselves at a crossroads: One path cries out for us to escape it all. The other calls us to persevere and lean on the Lord. Rather than merely survive, choose to abundantly thrive—by learning how to yield all control of your life to God, rest in His purpose and plan for your life, and enjoy the confidence of a heart wholly surrendered to Him.

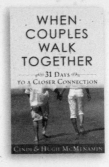

When Couples Walk Together
(with Hugh McMenamin)

Are the demands of everyday life constantly pulling you and your spouse in different directions? If you've longed to rekindle the intimacy and companionship that first brought you together, join Hugh and Cindi McMenamin as they share 31 days of simple, creative, and fun ways you can draw closer together again. You'll find your marriage greatly enriched as you experience anew the joys of togetherness and unselfish love.

Notes

1. Christian Counseling and Educational Services (CCES) reports 1 in 4 women will have a severe or major depression in their lifetime. For men it is 1 in 8. (See http://www.ccesonline.com/counseling/depression.htm#stats.)

2. It is estimated that 8 million Americans have an eating disorder—7 million women and 1 million men, according to the South Carolina Department of Mental Health. This department also reports 1 in 200 American women suffers from anorexia and 2 to 3 in 100 American women suffers from bulimia. (See http://www.state.sc.us/dmh/anorexia/statistics.htm.)

3. NASB.

4. For more on this concept of God redeeming your hurts into ways you can help others, see my book *When a Woman Overcomes Life's Hurts* (Eugene, OR: Harvest House Publishers, 2012).

5. You can learn more about Janet Thompson's ministry, About His Work, and her books at her website www.WomantoWomanMentoring.com.

6. 1 Kings 3:10-13.

7. For more on the ten steps to healing and wholeness, see my book *When a Woman Overcomes Life's Hurts*.

8. Second Corinthians 6:14 says, "Do not be yoked together with unbelievers. For what do righteousness and wickedness have in common? Or what fellowship can light have with darkness?"

9. Information about Moms in Prayer International and where to find a Moms in Prayer group near you (for moms of children in kindergarten through college) can be found at www.momsintouch.org.

10. This first appeared on Cheri Gregory's blog (http://cherigregory.com/blog/) on March 29, 2009.

11. Judges 6:15.

12. Leviticus 19:28.

13. Robert Jeffress, *Grace Gone Wild* (Colorado Springs, CO: Waterbrook Press, 2005), p. 41.

14. Jeffress, p. 43.

15. Janet Thompson, *Praying for Your Prodigal Daughter* (New York: Howard Books, 2007), p. 4.

16. 1 John 4:10-11 MSG.